POETRY FOR A LIFETIME

622-HERM

POETRY FOR A LIFETIME

Philip Vincent Hermida

To order additional copies of this book, contact:
Xlibris Corporation
1-888-7-XLIBRIS
www.Xlibris.com
Orders@Xlibris.com

CONTENTS

YOUTH

Horseshoe Bay 13
Tales of the Cemetery,
   or Charnel Knowledge 16
Ode to the Moon 19
Wanderings 22
Marblehead 27
My Date 28
Shark Heart 29
Lost Friends 30
All Alone 31
Years 32
The Die is Cast 33
Sere Winds 34
This is the Love 35
At the Door 36
Woodstock in Retrospect 37

ADOLESCENCE

Myth and Mystery 41
Requiem 49
Old Friend 50
I am an Empty Vessel 51
Now That You have
   Left Me 53

Complacent with Content 57
Evening Poem 61
Autumn Stream 65
Christmas 66
Early Snow 72
The Ocean 74
The Flowers of the Meadow Sing 84
Lame Reasoning 85

COLLEGE TIMES

College Times 89
Meditations with the Universal Self 91
The Martyr and the Prophet 94
The Marriage of Black and White 96
Written in Memory of a Lost Love 98
Narcissist 104
Walk 105
Ash 106
Part II 108
Part III 110

MATURITY

The Ghost Land 115
    Part I After the Burial 115
    Part II Living Monuments 117
    Part III On the Road to Heaven 122
Take Me to Forever 127
Where Bends Your Ways 129
Come Hither 130
Shoreline 132
That Girl There 133
Splendor in My Heart-Part I 134
Splendor in My Heart-Part II 136

Splendor in My Heart-Part III 144
The Tea Party 148
These Tears (for You) or This Little Box 160
Liberty Bell 161
When the Songbird Sings 163
Birthday Song 164
Father's Day 165

PEOPLE I HAVE KNOWN

Cheryl 169
To My Dear Vera 170
JoAnn's Place 172
Debbie 174
Moral on a Monday Morn 176
To Kate 178
Poem to Jenny 180
Look Before You Leap 187
Look Before You Leap (Revisited) 192
Roz 196
The M-Man 197
A Man and His Wink 198
Sonnet Inspired by Janet 199
Inspired by Janet 200
To _____ 201
Sweet Wonderful Sue 202
Oh Bonnie Sue 203
The Passing Years 205
My Peace 206

PHILOSOPHIES AND NATURE

Where It All Began 209
Sword and Pen 212
We Have Grown 213

Dawn 214
Midnight 215
Mother Nature 217
Rainbow Light and the Human Spectrum 221
Light I-Points of Light 223
Light II-When on This Earth We See Your Grace 224
Light III-Sometimes There's Plenty of It 225
Light V-Light with Your Magnetic Attractiveness 227
Eclectic I 229
Eclectic II 230
Eclectic III 231
Eclectic IV 232
Eclectic V 233
The Tide is High 234
Scythe of the Reaper 235
Sunset 237
Those Eyes 238
Audience 239
Milk the Breeze 240

DREAMS AND REMEMBRANCES

You Make Me Happy 243
Retreat 245
Id 246
Spanish Main 247
Sword in a Stone 248
Eternal Flame 251
Presence 253
Deep 254
What I Have Seen 255
Tears for Yesterday 256
From Mother to Son 257
Clouds 258
The Curse of Hathor 260

The Painted Desert 262
The Sorcerer's Incantation 264
Root 266
Laments 267
High Country 268
Frat Boy 269
The Chauvinist 270
From the Heart 271
A Simple Thought from Long Ago 272
Meeting in the Evening 273
The Spirit of Tutankhamen 275
Italian Ice 276
Nowhere 277
Parkway South 278

YOUTH

HORSESHOE BAY

In such idyllic splendor
We really aught to be
Sheltered from the ocean
By a cove of natural beauty,
This bay so majestically renowned
For its days without clouds,
All in all a most fabulous sight,
Attractive to both vacationers
And islanders alike.
Where neophytes go swimming
With scuba masks and snorkels
Those of more experience
Pull crabs from beneath the waters.
Anglers fish with long poles and lances,
The catches they throw back or give
To vacationers enjoying the local color.
Children play upon the beaches
Golden sunshine pours forth upon the bay
Painting the seawater aquamarine
Which cordially greets the happy bathers
Decked in pretty summer patterns.
Some bring lunches in a lunchbox,
Some a picnic basket, a big beach towel,
A barbeque, and a bottle of wine,
A perfect vacation, a perfect island.
The sand is pure and white,
No seaweed on the shore. The shoal protects
The swimmers from jellyfish with stingers.

A bright day lingers on this Bermuda High,
The sun is out to play,
The days are long and mellow,
Soft music in harmony with waves
Floats across the bay,
Beachcombers wade into the brine
No one here is pretentious
No one here is glum
The decorum is not garish
As a fire toasts a bun.
In this relaxing atmosphere
The rocky cliffs belay the ocean spray,
This afternoon the shallow water is balmy,
While later shadows roll across the shore
Day darkens into night, the basin glows
From algae, an eerie viridescence.
On the horizon a yellow moon sets
Here on a halcyon and humid eve
Over this tropical archipelago
Where the stars shine
And the Milky Way appears.
Of the jagged cliff some have fear
The natives though show bold abandon,
They dive fifty feet into the quiet liquid
Illuminated by a lantern.
These warm evenings
Gulls and pelicans bleat
Like sheep on the hills of Helicon.
Splashing in the water bathers
Frolic among the sea-plants
Where it is not too deep,
The entire cove is most compact,
Small in size, perhaps
One hundred feet in width.
By the entrance to the sea

Are the rocky heights
That earns this watery gem
Its famous name, "Horseshoe Bay."
Since then the years have flourished
With memories both poor and precious,
But from far away in mind it comes
These days of idle musing where
The years roll down the cataracts
Of nature's river Time.
So like the days at Horseshoe Bay
Such a long, long time ago
Will last these remembrances
In the minds of many visitors
Who come and go.
So here's to say good-bye
My friend, sweet meeting
Was our furlough;
These years have met with many beauties
Be it animal, vegetable, or mineral,
But when night comes throughout the years
And I lay myself to bed
I think of you, oh Horseshoe Bay
As a place I'd like to go
To see you once again
In all your glory, when at night you glow
Your eerie viridescence
That fades as the night draws on slow
Where I remember how
Upon the silky sand and rugged rock
On nesting birds and visitors alike
Your warm, soft, tender waters lapped.

TALES OF THE CEMETERY, OR CHARNEL KNOWLEDGE

Approach we make to yonder looming graveyard
Steadfast by the wayside sauntering past
Aspiring sedges bone dry as the path.
We sally forth obliged tonight to spend
With headstones, oblations among our friends.
By entrance through the gate we penetrate
The boundary of the gathered buried dead,
Bordered along all sides by vine entangled
Fences. A doleful mood begins descent
From the etheral sky nether meant
To permeate the atmosphere around
Our souls encumbered by remembrances
Whom we unwittingly promoted have
To giants greater than our mortal selves.
Now standing in such caskets are the hearts
Of buried hopes with unclaimed desire bred
Dragging on a healthy corpse of mundane knowledge
Atop the grassy plots blanketing their beds
These denizens of solitary berths
Interred in silence, reposed in sleeping earth
Unseen, unheard, unappertained withal.

Rise will they not but in us their only heirs
With testaments to epitaphs inscribed here
In darkness read by traces breathless spoke
While dire words are tipping from our tongues

A fire in our eyes is choked by smoke.
The moon has set, the sallow morning young
Has slowly grown dank with dropping dew,
Dampening our spirits once embolden
With tales of lore bucolic no forgotten.
Pierced to the quick our joints are aching stiff
Among the rank and file of white marble
Monuments entombed the tales of heroes
Left unsung, starlight shadows faintly cast
Across the fields of verdant mounds unmown,
We stealthily plod in keen humility
To the quiet bourn whispering we mourn
And find our seats upon a spire toppled.

In this time thwarting niche we often watched
The days of future passing, hardly noticed
Old tree branches grown barren towards the sky
Where energy fantastical creates
Heat lightning flashes across the clouded orb.
The leaves of wind whipped bush branches tingle
Against the rusting slatted iron fence.
Well into the deep eve hours recedes
The moon into densely thickening cover.
As the veins of the wood rise to the stars
The wind whispers increasingly sharply
Through the dirge whistling leaves. The squalls
Of ominous activity appear imminent
On gusty waves over this gramineous
Swale.

As the whitish light casts an empty haze
Through the dew like filaments of black and white
The lunar light is beaming bright
AS we go gathering under,
The air is clear, the stars are near

As we sit and watch in wonder,
The ever dead are in their bed
As the moonlight shadows cover
The darkness mourns the dead forlorn
In our song for ever after.

ODE TO THE MOON

Oh, moon, pale and gray, in the midnight sky
Casting shadows on the soft forest floor
Your lunar light shining bright
Ribbons of your moonlit orb
Float down from where you lay
Your silvery beams in the wood take flight
And fall upon an ancient mystic's door
Of a castle deserted standing high,
No traveler here has heard your lore
Of lover's love or wise men asking why.

Ye, half-moon, rising in the dusk of night,
Upon the heavens and upon the earth
Your quintessential glow and romantic light
Shine down in rivulets with magic rife;
The earth, the moon, the sun, and the stars
All in conjunction take to heights
As revelers ready with delights.

The evening grows, the light pervades
The busy streets, the ocean rough, and quiet glades.
Under the bower of pretty trees
The moonlit vales are covered with shades
Their amber light melts in the wind
Starlight droplets fall and fade
The climate warm this time of year
As your wan lips forever grin
Alone in the dark they have no fear

As they alight on branch and bough
And in a haze disappear
Upon the briars they did throw
Their wanton love from long ago.

With streams divine in laurel groves
Where eglantine and gooseberries grow
And on the church and steeple fraught
In icy winter's snow
With tradition and custom so
Falls the moonlight to and fro,
Love answers not to tragedy
Near the shadowy wood where lovers go.

So to ye, moon, with old landscape
Plays the tunes from days gone by
Under the leaves where darkness hides
Live the children the moon goddess knows
And around her aura a secret place
Only initiates can come inside
The works of man, the works of God
Cannot outdo the magic hand
That makes her fly in air so thin
As revelers dance and chant within.

No thought have they for tomorrow
Drunk on some elixir strong
For the night is all in one
A place that they can do no wrong
The only sight though setting soon
Is the surface of the moon,
And on a pilgrimage from far off land
They come to call and then are gone
In a frenzy great and grand

They return to daily life
'Tis the moon that they love now
Free from hate and free from strife.

WANDERINGS

I will stop by the warbling waters of the clearest streams
To hear the ever running onward of their dreams.
I will stare upon the placid pools of deepest lakes
Wondering ever upward your dreams to fill,
I will wander in the valleys and the rocky hills,
I will blunder in the darkness without your vision.
Cut down the highs, fill in the lows,
Smooth snowy icing on a cake of land,
No candles spark the match
I wish to see.

I met a princess by the freezing sea
Who spoke oracles of my life to me.
My words were few, but the thought was there,
She saw the sadness of my single stare.
By the torrents of eternal time
Shall you weep a solitary tear,
By the currents of discordant notes
Shall the empty hallways sing,
By the blessed path of simple dreams
Shall you choose the deep blue sea,
By the force of coldest will
Will you sink an empty well
While others wish upon the hills,
While others in the valleys dwell
Shall you hear deep tones
Echo in the empty shaft

That true love has given me.
The princess her eyes so dark they were
I wished to love anew, but only saw
The older flame was stronger still
Stronger than time vast,
Stronger than new beauty fair,
Stronger is the memory of awe,
Strongest is her cutting kill.

My long life I know will last,
But once I had true love to dare,
Dare I did, but only I did scare
My love from the bower of care,
My love from the wisdom of soul,
My love from the apple of God,
My love from the wine of His blood,
My love from a beautiful life.

How long will burn the flame
That on Olympus burned?
That on a gravestone etched
Marks out a plot of land
Where a house's home might stand
That marks the love of life.

How long will last that thought
Through morning, noon, and night,
Through spring, summer, and fall,
Throughout the timeless years
In the fishes in the mountain lakes,
In the songs of woodland birds,
In the ducks and golden geese,
In the seekers of the Golden Fleece?

From the rising of the dawn
To the setting of the moon,
From the blushing of a rosy cheek
To the wane of fitful sleep,
I will hold the thought in my heart dear,
I will spell the word in every tongue;
The thought will last 'til words be mum,
The thought will come every day,
The thought will turn me inside out,
The thought will turn me outside in,
The thought will bid me call your name,
The thought will tear my hair
From a head that has one thought to think.

What gift is this that I may know
No thought will there ever be
That leads not to your door?
Though every path adds to the maze
And every new soul may amaze,
Know every path seeks out your door
In every life there is a tale
That's tapping, knocking, scratching at your door.

When I knock upon your door
And bid you tell me from the heart
I hear the door is locked to me,
And when I hear your heart is locked
Then, I know who is the key,
The key to your first door
The key to every door in heart,
The key to every door in store
To every dream you see
The key your heart must seek
If you ever hope to be free.

May free souls fly to Heaven's gate
In pairs upon angelic wing
May each be each other's key.
When I alone approach the sky,
I hear a voice behind me cry,
"Wait for me my precious key!"
But, then I see the voice's source:
A lonely rock, my sight beholds
The only rock for me.

The rock speaks out in hardened tones,
"I've got to be free
I've got to have room,
I speak a stern voice,
Stay away from me."

Then, a tree answers,
"The things you do
With no place to go,
Love you don't make
Only hearts your break."

And the tree continued,
"Oh, little rock,
Oh, pretty rock,
Come burning sun,
Come freezing rain,
I call my plea,
Please answer me."

The rock's last words were,
"You are no good
For the better is better,
The better is good,

But the good is better,
For better
For worse
Forever."

MARBLEHEAD

Sunrise at dawn
The ocean is calm
The ship in a fog
In the distance a horn.

Noon on the seas
Sailboats in fair wind
Tack from the shore
And a boat race begins.

Sunset at night
The moon rules the sky
Sailors look far and wide
A ship waits for high tide.

Midnight the waters
Are dark and are deep
Near the bay boats are anchored,
The foghorn repeats.

MY DATE

My date
She was so womanly
With her eyes blue as the sky,
Her cheeks peaches, her skin cream,
And her hair shining raven sable as the night
In a midsummer's dream.
She ruled all the men
Upon which she came
Dressed in golden splendor
In her boudoir of renowned,
Her friends could not keep track
Of her dates with rich men
From the far corners of the earth
They came seeking marriage,
But she had other ideas
On the other side of town.

SHARK HEART

My tears are cold
In my white shark heart
Upon the sheets
I fold.

The bait has made
My emotions soft,
In my intentions hard
I burst forth
Upon her face.

A kiss from the past
On my cheek expression wrought,
On my white shark heart
Her image was embossed.

I feel love
Where none exists
I cry out
My shark heart
Exploding,
I am beached upon the shore
Of humanity's ocean.

LOST FRIENDS

When all your friends are long gone
Somewhere your ex is laying on her lawn
Knowing she does not give a darn
Anymore.

When all your friends have left you
Somewhere your ex is laying in the dew
Knowing too her friends number few,
But her boyfriend is with her every day
Knowing she does not care for me
Anymore.

When all your friends are out having fun
And you are just waiting for the day to be done
Somewhere your ex thinks off and on
Of you far away at home long and gone.
I try not to wonder what she thinks
Anymore.

ALL ALONE

All alone the night is long
Without love to keep you going.
Playing in the lonely hearts of lonely friends
Far away and removed from me
Is time and distance separating us.

YEARS

They come and go like the wind
Upon shifting sands on shores unknown.
The years will eat me up and lay me low.
How many summer suns have I to see?
How many winter moons have come and gone?
Eternity awaits us my love to meet again
In future lives unknown I see ahead
Drifting upon the waves of chance for us.

THE DIE IS CAST

Come back my first and we shall last
To love anew whilst life is young
Where many have in others sought
Like warriors who have vainly fought
With thunder 'gainst a lighting bolt,
When wax is soft and newly pressed
Into a mold it will take shape,
But wax once cold will harden fast
And hold the form the die has cast.

Thus, in my heart my love is fixed
Not by my will which I love not,
But by a flame of greater heat
To melt an idol blows won't beat
Ablaze into a warming felt
While still your flame is pure chaste white
There shall not beam a brighter light,
But hearts that burn with hottest ire
Broadcast "no dice" for prime desire.

SERE WINDS

A nova's power super once will wane
And every morn awaits her dawn to pass,
Every seed's bloom will bloom in fresh flowers
When everyone is leaves, but few do last
To will us both sere winds of fortune blown
Into life's past as all have passed before
Preserving thy beauty with but words to show.

THIS IS THE LOVE

This is the love I've waited for so long
That always will be strong
And never come to wrong
Don't say it's been too long
For me to now return
To play in every song this is the love.

This is the love of a melody
That never played as sweet
A melliferous treat
As I will ever meet
These lonely days I keep
Until I touch you, treat, this is the love.

AT THE DOOR

My old girlfriend was at the door
To see if she could hear me snore
The guards they found her lurking there,
"I won't do it again I swear."
"Let her go," said I, "Woe,
It's my old girlfriend head to toe."
"Why didn't you let her in," my wife grinned,
Are you kidding, you'd have me skinned.

"My, what are you doing here
In the darkness, oh, so near?
Stand in the light so I can see your face."
"I'm leaving now in steadfast haste.
I take leave of your home, cross-country I go,
With you and your friend I don't want a row."

WOODSTOCK IN RETROSPECT

Down on Yasgur's farm, back in Sixty-nine
The masses came a rollin' through the wide-mouth gate
And when the day laid down, and out had stalked the night
The masters of the throng n'er had seen such a sight
Children of the flowers, Yippies, Hippies, one and all
Poured upon those pastures, a new age grown tall
Then the amps were turned up, strings were tuned to key
Red-eyed new messiahs wa-wa'd in history
While all the wide-eyed laity wallowed in debris
The Airplane at apogee and Hendrix at his peak
Launched a NASA satellite to far-out spacey freaks
Crosby, Stills, and Nash were young, the Who were still in town
Sunshine flew the highest with feet in fenny ground
Orange balls of fire, white lightning case by case
What wonder some remember they even saw the place
Flat on a back in a bottomless tent
To placate the howls of angry foment
For miles around you could hear the bash
Of revelers hankering o'er a stash
Or skinny-dippers bathing with abound
In cans of worms beards and long hair for a crown,
And dodgers burned draft cards to strains of, "Hell no."
In last summer's disruption of the Chicago convention
The Panthers were prancin', the ghettoes in riot
Ere Nixon announces the majority's silent
In those late days of campus unrest

And civil rights marches to the White House steps
For Kennedy's Camelot laid in his grave
Sank that utopian vision, a Hyannis Port wave,
Gunned down in the hindsight of nostalgic digression.

ADOLESCENCE

MYTH AND MYSTERY

Red lips have read into our hearts
Love, beating to a quicker beat
When we embrace beauty, the love
Of beauty's favors with its flavors
Makes our lives go 'round the world
Searching for love.
A pair of lips part
Tasting the sweet, succulent
Fruit like the parts of a pear
Divided with a knife that cuts
Through the red tape
Of budding buttercups
That lets love flower
Into glorious bouquets.
Long flowing hair combed
Like a honeycomb
Around a lovely face
Like a picture hung on
The words of her melodious voice
On the tip of my tongue, her words
Beautiful words, with a tip
Of advice by which to remember her.
Her cream complexion
Sweet and smooth, full bodied
Her eyes azure, the votes
Are for her, the "ayes" have it.
Her eyelashes long as I long
To see her eyelashes

Looking at me long ago, looking
At her, her model figure
In a figure of speech
Pure as the thriven snow,
And modest, with youth robust
And full of life, like a silver chalice
Overflowing with wine, her wine
Like a magic drink to fall in love.
To fall in love in the fall,
The harvest fall, to harvest love,
The wine to hear her whine
Floating on the breeze into a new season
To discover sensationalist sensations
Or to discover the spice of life
The spice of love. The spice
Of the new season's seasonings
Brings variety into our lives
When so many are left without love
In the winter while so many are right
To be patient, the new season
Springs a new spring garden,
Garden of our soul when flowers
Spring into our hearts
Giving birth to new romance
In our minds and not to mind
So many fluttering wings of chance
Flattering the wind.
Our lives flying by with opportunities
Watching the time go by on our watch
Waiting for the right moment,
Hoping we will not be left
Without love for another year.
Watching tears fall
While others seem happy and gay,
Watching the teardrops of Heaven

Rain in the spring.
Monarchs reign over dominions
While we rein in our emotions
Like reeling in a line
Like a line of fishing tackle
Is reeled in with a fish
As a line of poetry reels
In a lost soul.
To read among the reeds
Of a summer pond,
Verse, to diversify our minds,
To enjoy entertainment, our readers
Enter our poems, to feel feelings,
To emote on emotions,
Our listeners who listen to spoken words
Speak their piece about shattered pieces
Of their lives
Hoping to find peace of mind,
Like a gold mine in words on a page
Written to page thoughts deeply buried
To piece pieces together
Like a puzzle to make life
More a mystery than a misery.
Throughout the years and hours of our lives
When around the clock the year passes
Each season is another seasoning
Of the spice of life.
And many passes being made
By many people throughout the past,
Present, and future,
To present themselves as eligible
To the attractive, to provide
Themselves with the trappings
Of winners in this race through time
To love before the world grows

Too old and cold to provide
Love anymore.

Remember those days in youth
When love was a mystery, like
Clouds that block the sun,
Or like a fog on a misty country road
That dissipates as the morning drives along,
The mystery of her with her beauty in your heart
Those splendid days you took heart
With splendid love lapping on the shores
Of your life. Those rare moments
Like finding diamonds in the sand
Upon the beach of life's ocean,
The ocean of humanity where grains
Of sand are the multitudes.
Across the seas, oceans of emotions
Rise and fall on the caprice of her words
Her beauty elating and deflating
The dispositions of men's nature.
Remember those days of simple love
Together in a car in a lover's lane,
Together climbing mountains of desire,
Together besides a fire, the fire of passion,
Together at the beach under a blanket
Of sweet talk, together in love.
Remember the dreams of youth
When your spirit ran free in the forests long ago,
And as you grew so grew your dreams
That these moments might be yours
Moments of happiness, pleasure, and love.
When these dreams were fulfilled
They became dreams again
Dreaming that love would return.
So in years, like tears that roll

Down the face of the cliffs of time
May we all have dreams,
Dreams fulfilled and dreams
Of the future answered by the sweet
Sound of a pretty woman
Fresh in personality like
A maiden unfolding like
The bud of a flower in May
And may that flower bloom
Into a life fulfilled, filled
With the nectar of satisfaction
And may love fulfilled
Garner your life with happiness,
A love of life and a life of love.
Also, may you see the beauty
Of nature's artistic hand
Like when she painted in the sky
A double rainbow whose awe
And majesty filled half the hemisphere
With brilliant color, intensified
By the rarified Coloradan air,
Gargantuan in size repeating
Light's spectrum twice over, inspiring
These words that you may hear
Spoken years down the road
Written in books read
Generations from today
Whereas that mighty rainbow
Enduring in memory, lasted only moments
Evanescent, however, its intensity
Transcending that of any other
Vision ever seen.
Remember the dreams of youth
The dreams that flow free
Like a mountain stream

That meanders down a mountainside
Into vales and dales
Of fertile young minds
Ready to learn the ways of the world;
And may these streams nourish
Orchards that flourish
With bountiful fruit:
Fruits in the heart, wonderful to see
And delicious to taste,
May your labor here produce
Worthy fruits, the fruits of love,
Fruits of the womb.

Fruits of the womb
In the future will come to reap
Dividends in the end, when snows
Are on the mountain peaks
And the spark of life is waning
From your veins and silvered hair
Is all upon your pate, when
Slow and infirm you prate,
Sedate and quiet your becoming
In years across your prow
When every day seems hazy,
Not at wits end, as often greets
The young, but content.
You agree you are lucky
Your progeny will live
And bear your name and memory
With windy days behind
And wrinkles on your brow,
Whether the years have been kind
Or not to your soul
It will retain its value.
When you are on that homestretch

With it all behind you now
On the lonely marl
Or with moil still to come
Whether you are rich or poor
It's still a cinch
To say there is a door
Back into a world of yore.
So spin a yarn and call it fun
Recall when life had just begun,
Think of a farm
That harbors the old
In from the breeze
That spoils the young.
Gifts from the meek
The shallow do not seek
The years travel on in blue and gold
While purple clouds fill the sky
No need to ask why,
Remember the sun
With warmth does it come
The years will abade
Insatiable greed
So here's to the wise
Both old and new
If you have found here a cue
Take heart in what's true
Many are the tricks of the past,
Hold on to your hand
Hold on and hold fast
There is more to our heirs
Than the youth who are rash.
So if you're still with us
After such a long time
Perhaps in your heart
There still is a lass

Or a bonnie beau from long ago
A moderate voice to quell your fear
That you will be lost in another year
There are things in this world we do not know
To find them we have to look far
Into the heavens beyond any star.

REQUIEM

In life we love
In death we mourn
The loss of loved ones
Now departed
From our sight,
But not our hearts.
Sometimes
We make new starts,
With others
We feel near,
But our friends
Or family
Now in the ground
We still think are dear.
A headstone on a grave
Or urn upon the shelf
Is all that is left,
His or her wealth
Bequeathed by will
And testament
May fill
The emptiness we feel
By loss of life,
So let us heal
The wounds of grief,
And hope the pain is brief.

OLD FRIEND

A hot toddy quickly melted the icy years
Since we had last met.
We weaved words of welcome and friendship
Across the gulf of time that had separated us.
We are older now with snow over our eyes
And barren fields on our heads,
It seemed like centuries had passed,
But our thoughts were not slower
Nor our wits dimmer.
We recalled many events, which had transpired
In that time long ago, referring
To them as, "The old days."
In our sentimental conversation the old days
Came to life again with stories
Of love and war—both good and bad,
Tipping on our tongues with the brightness
Of our minds and the spirit
Of camaraderie that always piqued
Our get-togethers.
The hour grew late,
Our favorite pub about to close,
We said our good-byes and plunged
Into the liquid darkness of the night
Still friends, not knowing
If we'd meet again.

I AM AN EMPTY VESSEL

I am an empty vessel
My bucket is unfull
I skip along a nature walk,
And listen for her fill.

Through all the stucco missions
Through all the arid sands
The spirit I am missing
Engenders the Rio Grande.

I am an empty vessel
Sweet Sirens are no fill
They leave the heavens empty
As do a heartless crew.

I've stood on banks of rivers
With walls of rainbow hue
To sight a distant vista
Where beauty might be true.

I am artistic vision
Without a marble arch
I mock with aged derision
What moderns pass as art.

I am Osiris setting
Across a tabletop
Where ageless sands are shifting
To find a better spot.

I am Caesar toasting
Victory in Gaul
Yet I am not a-boasting
Of Cleopatra's fall.

I am a candle's tallow wax
Embossed with a signet's face
I am spun threads of golden flax
Weaved into royal lace.

I am tomorrow's harbinger
The Harpies have cast down
I am Mercury's messenger
By Venus yet unfound.

I am eternal restlessness
Of unrequited love
And say my end is hopelessness
Without your nesting dove.

NOW THAT YOU HAVE LEFT ME

Now that you have left me
Now that I am gone,
Who shall always love me
Ever and anon.

With endless time a-passing
Wherever seed is sown
The ageless rock is crying
Your heart is hard as stone.

All of mankind's ocean
All the human sea
Begs for the emotion
Long concealed in thee.

Long I this have pondered
Old my soul has grown
Far as I have wandered
I love you alone.

You're a hope chest plundered
I'm a hollow soul
I'm a genie bottled
You're a stopperd hole.

You, my star, have fated
Fortune signed and sealed

In testament of hatred
No heir to you appealed.

Storm the angry heavens
Roiled long by thunder
Lightning strikes a virgin
Once a vestal wonder.

Heart I thought I knew you,
But you were out to prove
No one could see through you
To view you, veil removed.

Asunder are we broken
Halves without one whole
Heart you are unspoken
Ashes choke your soul.
Priceless living riches
All humanity
Netted are we fishes
I am one for thee.

Spirit you inspire
Youth's charm; jollity,
Sun, imbued with fire
Nourishes vert finery.

I'm a sunken treasure
You're a pirate's hold
Darkest depths unmeasured,
Unfathomed waters cold.

Say you do not love me
Say you are untrue
Who will at last replace me
And be as good as new?

Batten down the hatches
Sail no more unfurled,
No matter all the catches
Were oysters now unpearled.

Femme-fatale you've finished
All who came to stay
Claiming you were oddish
In your customary way.

Someplace there's a girl who loves me
Far or near she's n'er alone
Somewhere there's a girl who hates me
Whom she loves she will not own!

Happy or sad, she's always mad
Because her true love is not sin
Who or what, it be not had
In good or bad, in frown or grin.

Some love many, some love one,
But n'er have I e'er heard of any
That never loved any but none,
Despite a traumatic memory.

All my lettered unanswered
All of my calls unreturned
All of my plans uncreated
From the inception inurned.

All of your love still unaltered
All in one image is spurned
Graven or God, virtue faltered
And fell to invectives affirmed.

In couplets, quartets, poem, or prose
I dedicate eternally
A flame from ashes that arose,
My love, you live immortally.

You may rant you do not want it,
And rave it means nothing to you,
The longer you stay pitched to fight it
The longer it stays stuck in you.

Try as you may, try as you might
With my eyes you will not part
As surely as I pass from sight
So long as I remain your heart.

COMPLACENT WITH CONTENT

Complacent with content
To write these paltry rhymes
The chimes of bells have sent
Into so many minds.

I am a living man
Now twenty-two in age
The muse that moves my hand
Is three years on her page.

Beauty is everywhere
The wish to love I balk
At is by far compare
More color than white chalk.

Whose arms will bear the fruit
For that fair maiden made
She a lyre or a lute
And like a mystic played.

Now the sea is battering
Shoals and the open sky
There a pelican clattering
While gulls o'er lonely fly.

On the gap of the infinite sea
I still dream of an infant song,

"Bring back my bonnie to me,"
For an Irish lass I once longed.

Or an Irish castle to be
On the banks of the river Mind
Still fresh the branches on my tree
That spring leaf left in ten years time.

When I was six years in the snows
I skied in the back of my yard
Long with dear Paula's runny nose
Ere my mother fed birds with lard.

I scorched my feet in July
Plunged in the water, a flash
From the sands at the pool of the Y,
In the sun of my summers past.

We played in the marsh and the pond
And dammed our mud to the streams
And talked on in dreams of life beyond
Oozings through toes and Patty's screams.

One day the mallards went away
No more to quack at six o'clock
Because she fed them twice a day
Out of duty, my mother's stock.

We ran in the fields of our dreams
The days of our youth were as free
As milky weed seeds in sunbeams,
Or Skipper and John in a tree.

Now bound to the strand of the shore
By the waves of the rising tide

Though greed is desire for more
The curious search far and wide.

Meadowlark by the pompous grass
Tanager in the apple tree
One single fleeting moment fast
Why such a lasting memory?

Ruby red tulips once were planted
Under the cups of the dogwood
By these my new springs I counted
'Til anon they no longer stood.

Anthill behind the dirt pile,
My father choked with chlorodane;
On his shoulders I a smile
Lifeless hill tree stump-like remains.

The portulacas burning red,
Spreading like a wildfire,
Brimming o'er the rock garden bed,
Shade grown long made them retire.

Forsythias around the front
Were in their golden yellow bloom
'Til a frost shriveled the year's font,
Skated on the lawn that afternoon.

It was the spring of Sixty-six
Barbara brought pussy willows in
To second grade our eyes to fix
Upon nature with beauty trimmed.

Muse, hand of memory taken
Through coves, not of unmixed waters,

Do not think I am mistaken
Though memory imagination borders.

All these childhood memories
Are vivid, visionary thoughts
When occurrences yesterday
Are dross reminders of lost hearts.

And now I close another night's parade
Wishing upon the east at break of day
To find you waiting in a vernal glade,
Take me, or with another your life stay.

EVENING POEM

As the last fire of the sun ceases for the day,
The naked moon appears in nightly display
Playing on the hearts and in the dreams of lovers
Upon the mossy clearings of forest bowers,
I drive along the crowded, hectic roadway
As the others all seem to be going today
To meet their friends or relatives this eve
As old men read papers and spinsters weave
A blanket or a sweater for their nieces,
A skein of yard from the wool of many fleeces.
In the early evening air of autumn season
Some begin to understand the rhyme and reason
So many pass this way but then forget
Why an irksome life is no excuse to fret.
There are so many areas to excel,
And everyone has a chance at doing well,
And though it's true you can't beat city hall
There still is room for lovers one and all.
On the radio a favorite tune does play
Reminding us of good times yesterday
Like that blonde haired girl who once struck me funny
She would have made me such a lovely honey
When the bees of springtime were flying in the field
The onslaught of enlightenment at times does yield
A somber tone and demeanor seemingly profound
Upon the soul and personality around
The grounds of higher learning institutions
Where students study life and constitutions,

And are trained to manage society
With calm attitude and sobriety.
In this or any other country there are some
Who see through the ages when the day is done
Or believe in spirits of the past,
And say slow down do not go fast
Or you will miss the meaning of the night;
To them I say you've seen the light,
And others by the thoughts on which they fly
Appear to work hard at everything they try,
But often fail at labors arduous
Because they are always in a terrible rush
To complete a daily set of tasks or other
With goals that have been set by another,
But with dreams in their heads that are unending
I compliment them in their persevering
And wish all the best in work and love
Hoping they find their dreams a cut above
Those poor souls who to their dying day
Are brokenhearted and can only pray
Their rewards are beyond the grave
While every day they slave and slave
For a little piece of relaxation
Which all too often goes without mention.
So when the time comes to lay it all on the line
Put your best foot forward in the daily grind
The rat race as it's called so often apropos
Spending your life always on the go
Caught in the workplace time after time
Lying to yourself that you feel fine
With no place to hide but an empty home
Where memories live and die when old we've grown
Across this country and its continent
Which upon occasion breeds discontent
Among the ranks of the youth in unemployment

Now turned to computers for enjoyment
With which you can see the entire world
From your living room or den so I am told.
Attention to the facts and details
In any endeavor certainly entails
A great amount of effort and comprehension,
So to those great minds with apprehension
I should like to say I once felt as you
That it is difficult to see a project through
To its conclusion with certain benefit
With words of advice to whomever wants it
I say hang tough and be aloof
May your accomplishments be your proof
That you can run with the best of them
That are you peers among fellow men.
Do not allow setbacks to slow you down
In any field one must be profound
Set your goals within your scope of knowledge,
And go to the most prestigious college
It will be to your advantage in future business
And afford you much respect and happiness
Perched above your desk that proverbial sheepskin
Such a great asset when you try to win
A promotion in all avenues of competition
In which you will be immersed after graduation.
So tread not lightly on your laurels
Sink your teeth into those morsels
Seize the moment, seize the power
It may be your finest hour
Play it cool, play it by ear
Concentrate on one particular career,
And in the long run you'll be accorded
A position of influence most lauded.
Thus, in conclusion we most certainly may say
Though there seem many obstacles in the way,

While many offer prayer to God or country
You must take the bull by the horn of plenty,
Success is not without some sacrifice
The first that goes is often a social life,
And many of your friends so nice
Will leave you like a block of ice,
For some this is too great a price to pay,
And I for one have found it to be this way,
I opted for a life of ease of sorts,
But remember when it comes to such reports
One cannot dismiss the facts so true
With my knowledgeable words what one can view
Seek peace of mind in anything you do
Because in your heart you'll find contentment too
So when you find what you are seeking through and through
Just keep your secrets secret, and show some rue.

AUTUMN STREAM

Over the bounding brook we go,
Over the gurgling stream
Of many cool days of autumn sun
And many a merry moment I dream.

The colored leaves of trees fall down
On the rushing stream and wood,
And in the forest we play all day
In the fall of our childhood.

Sometimes the rain beats down in sheets,
Sometimes the wind does whip
The animals, they run and hide
When we hop and skip.

The days grow shorter and the birds fly
In the clear blue skies above,
School time comes and we say good-bye
To the woodland stream we love.

Another year has come and gone
With our lessons and our letters glum
Until this season's finished and done
And we can think once more of fun.

In that bower thick with fern and frond
Blithe, quiet times we'll find
In future days of life so fond
When the fresh stream comes to mind.

CHRISTMAS

'Tis the Christmas season again this year
Bringing warm greetings from out of the cold
Hoping to meet you with glee and good cheer
A tradition of joy and happiness old
With season's greeting and barrels of fun
To think of friends present and past
Turning a new leaf when the New Year's begun
Amazed at how time moves so fast
May next year bear peace and goodwill
Into our hearts with love to fill.

Oh, Christmastime the joy of you
Does really give me such a thrill
And when I think of you so true
I rise above with iron will
To prove again your worthiness
In these words of eloquence
Peace on earth in happiness
Goodwill to men so earnest
Who their life did sacrifice
As martyrs to the name of Christ.

We celebrate the Lord's birthday
In reverence and devotion
In Bethlehem so far away
A symbol of salvation
And when Christ promised eternal life
And prophesied His death

There was upon the earth much strife
With crucifixion and thorny wreath,
But to this day He still does live
In Heaven above with love to give.

Three wise men bearing gifts came by
To that manger on the edge of town
Led by a star that shone on high
With Joseph there and Mary bound
For the road to Galilee
The river Jordan then did stream
And refuge there promised safety
The star on them still did beam
And others saw it far away
And said the Lord is born this day.

So long ago the story told
In divers ways and divers lands
In languages both new and old
When Mary held Him in her hands
The angels there did come and go
The son of man's nativity
For all to see for all to know
Had come to pass in that country
The Promised Land of Israel
With Jerusalem and Jericho.

Now in this modern day and time
The meaning of Christmas is often lost
The modern world is often blind
Fighting over land and cost,
But still a tree and still a church
Upon the streets does signify
And helps the pious in their search
Their sins and wrongs to rectify

Gone to mass on Christmas Eve
A time to worship and believe.

Upon the apse on Christmas morn
Sang the choir true and grand
Christ the Lord this day is born
Praise be to Him in every land
May He be with us in our prayers
Wishing our souls for Him to keep
Absolve our guilt and vain desires
Glory to Him our toils to reap
Lord of Lights and Lord of Hosts
Father, Son and Holy Ghost.

So Christmastime is here again
With lights and tinsel on the tree
Everyone a gift, everyone a plan
Me for you and you for me
Christmas day with children happy
Is a sight we like seeing
Apropos of wise men's glory
At His right hand grace receiving
High up where angels sing
And cherubs fly and seraphs wing.

Midnight mass in a basilica
On Christmas Eve soon here
In this the Golden Age of America
Will ancient wisdom soon make clear
The ancient fathers of the faith
Free from harm and circumstance
Did their thinking not in haste,
And has the privilege to enhance
The depth and knowledge of Catholicism
With Rosary and catechism.

Glory to God in the highest
Christ the Lord is born this day
To all who are a theist
Thou shalt find God this way
The light of Heaven shines above
On Christmas we observe His birth
His sermon and His love
For all Mankind brought forth
The master and the Lord we serve
That our absolve may never swerve.

Our spirit so he does inspire
Since Moses on the mount was seen
A burning bush on fire
Unconsumed by sin unclean
Now in this day so far from then
In the Gospels it is written
By four Apostles and their pen
Of them it is said quite often
They were chosen from the beginning
To them on Christmas make an offering.

The years have come the years have gone
And now there dawns a new millennium,
But still the will of Christ is strong
And keeps the laity from Satan's poison
The soul of man has been redeemed
And now the Advent once more comes
Which soon will ring up once undreamed
Two thousand years of time that runs
Into the course of history
With grace and magnanimity.

So, thus, we say of Christmastime
May the Lord be with you every day

Whether troubles brew or all is fine
Wishing you good tidings in every way
That peace and harmony are yours
Throughout the coming holidays
With a holly wreath upon your doors,
And cheer throughout the New Year always
With good friends and good times to come,
And a friendly spot to rest when the day is done.

May Christmastime find you happy
Knowing someone cares
About you and friends so aptly
Driven to His cause
Expressed in poetry most deeply
In philosophy and religion
For those so prettily
Thriven to reaction
On history or love
Or to the Lord above.

So may the light of Christ
Shine on you one and all
May you be free from strife
Come this and every fall
Christmastime again is here
The season of lights and giving
Making gay the weather drear,
And I hope you are receiving
Some gifts from those you cherish
And remember, believe in Him, and you shan't perish.

So make this Christmas special
For someone who is fond,
And to you is partial,
And form a special bond

That lasting through the years
Will make life less severe,
And won't bring you to tears
Though things may be austere
The Christmas season is upon us,
Thus, for you I'll make a fuss.

EARLY SNOW

A breath of wind in the cool evening air,
A rush in the twilight is heard,
A voiceless rush into the atmosphere
Through the window invisible.
The wind blows only trees,
Vibrant embers crack on fire,
I cannot see into the thick darkness
Invisibly indivisible, invariably
In the wind the snow dusts the earth
And leaves a wasteland in the night.

The clouds lift, fog dissipates
The stars light up like neon out on Broadway
Bright children running through the snow,
Over the air we go into the storm
Ideas float upward in my brain.

The titanic forces of nature
Communicate to form living things
These mystifying nights and morns
Dismal, dank, and misty as the sea
Broken on the rocks and jagged edges
Are another man's hopes and dreams
Sunk to the bottom of the tidal basin
As the wind rushes off in delight.

When the tenebrous darkness turns into day
Sweet, silent sounds are all that's left

The day rushes in like rush hour traffic
The stars are gone after another sleepless,
Profligate night.

THE OCEAN

In a dance
The shorebirds gull
My mind to prance
And mull
In belief
I hear a voice
Offering relief
And a choice
To meet her again
Not on a bitter beach,
But on a pleasant strand
My heart to reach
Down deep in the water
And with anticipation
To await her.

Oceans of emotions
Roll across the sand
Mixing ideas of love
In admiration grand
Although feeling despair
In the salt sea air
Listening to the endless refrain
Of the surf's perpetual roar.

On the pier
In yesteryear
With her

The situation
Sink or swim
I took a chance
Her love to win
I did cast
Acting fast,
But another fish
Made off
With the catch.
Still harboring
Imagination
With baited breath
She spoke
In the crowded gulf port
Making a joke
About a news report
On the docks
Where cold sea breezes dampen
The party atmosphere
Lit by a Chinese lantern.

On the jetty at morning
In the saltwater
Fresh bread they are pouring
Where fishermen crab
With block and tackle
In overalls drab
While I am sitting
On that jetty
Of eagerness
Without such thoughts petty
Nor with imposition
Awaiting a ship
Of friendly disposition.

Docked
For the meeting
Of two imposing souls
Fishing for a meaning
In the schools
Upon which knowledge
Trolls.

I embark
Upon a voyage
Returning before dark
I send a message
Addressed to her from me,
"Seasick as a dog
A sailor never be
Sick to death with failure
Loathing to dream lonesomely."

Stoic to endure
Vacations on this sandy rime
Thinking of the past or future
In great distances of time
One swept away
By the waning tide
Of a memorable day,
The other with the incipient
Ebbing
Expectations
Of another year
Of ocean harvest
In seawater cool and clear.

These insipid moments
Drag on into hours
Leaving seashore apartments

With nearby ocean flowers
The sand is scorching hot
Under the sun—suntan
Pineapples in the clay pot,
Then with hazy weather
Snuffing out the heat
Next to the briny breakers
Surfboarders cannot beat
Ends a short relationship
In tropical doldrums
When into somnolence we slip.

The curtain of nighttime
Falls on
Today's romantical musical,
But loud music plays
Onward in my mind
Across the harbor
Motorboats at bay
Sailfish owners
Hesitating,
They drink brews
As a storm brews.

The sky turning ominous
I peer across the sea
A waterspout dangerous
Which we all agree
Suggests that we are lost
In the understanding
Of the human cost
The forces of lost love
Governing the ages
While rain falls from above
On the empty pages

Of the minds of youth
Have swayed by windy rages
Nature's angry truth.

Waves of thought
Upon the seashore
Pound decisiveness
And surety
Broken on the coral reefs
By dissipation
Of hurricane energy,
But unaging effort
And responsibility
Rescues emergencies
Of shipwrecks
And flounderings
At sea.

Arriving on the airwaves
To the sights of troubadours
With tambourines performing
Among a jolly crew
This airborne ship
Has made it through
Last night's storm,
A radar blip,
Having landed
In an ocean paradise
Each to his own device.

Greetings ostentatious
Opulent, splendorous
Abodes, all along the sea
Once in a far off land,
Now new homes on the lea.

Birds portray
A happy image
And our fears allay
The good weather
Not a mirage
On this merry day
Pelicans dive for dinner
Near our restaurant
A gourmet winner,
We dine out
In colored beauty
Flowers and palms
Bedeck the scenery.

I'm certainly not
In the mood
For any sort of food
I just ate
A big plate
Of frog's legs
From outer space.

A lighthouse overlooks
The horizon, landward
Blows the wind, ships
Head for the open sea
Laden with rich spirits.

We have arrived in pleasure land:
Trample on the trampoline
Throw the beach ball
Catch it with your hand
Running in the hall
Sleeping in the heat
No bugs to bite

No socks on foot
With fish from the sea
And greenery
Water in cisterns
By the bay,
A plane flies away.

Tile roofs,
And bread loaves,
Scuba gear,
Swim trunks
On the chair,
Flippers
In the closet,
Like a porpoise guiling
Dolphins of disguise
In the skies
Danger lurks
Not far away,
But they are unaware.

Can you guess the nature
Of this troller we have towed
Or would you say Atlantis
Is on the Devil's Triangle road?

Somewhere death haunts the day
As remembering
Haunts my mind
Like spirits lost at sea,
Or an underwater gold mine
The hearty soul abandon
All is lost, all is dross
Pantina on the statue
Scoria to one and all

All tossed in the ocean
Under seaweed and debris.

Now homeward bound
The only sound
The wake of water
On the bow
A close call in how
In retrospect
As it is now
Of those times
There were crimes
Of conscience
Acted out in mime,
But I write
With delight
To that poet blind
To feel the light
Of the yellow orb
And absorb
The heat of love
From realms above
This tiny isle,
With a smile
On our faces
With those traces
Of beauty
From the golden ages.

Waking dazed
At morning
We contemplate
And anticipate
Expecting good
To come

From above
With legions
Heavenly
Led by angels,
But the only angels
I see
Are dead.

Drowned in sorrow
With no end in sight
I wish for tomorrow
I feel no fright
With magic
That will see me
Through the night,
The worst and best
Yet to come
I remember the first
Day it began,
But now
Broken down
Shades on the ground
Seen by one and all
Soon to be
Buried at sea.

Heavy going
On the rough ocean
Bobbing in the swells
Searching for a notion,
Here the porpoise dwells,
And apprehends
The gods are right
No end in sight
These hard days

Of burden and blight
Upon the strong
Right or wrong
Caress the sky
You wise guy
Take a wight,
Making love is all
This world has to offer.

THE FLOWERS OF THE MEADOW SING

The flowers of the meadow sing
The coming of an early spring
A flock of birds comes reeling in
To see a bevy of fish swim round a brim
A lily pond where the frogs croak slow
And a snapping turtle stands out stout.
The stoic forces work their way on me
On the lucid airs of jollity.
Nature's fauna cajole me right
My love, she is nowhere in sight,
But I don't mind beneath this pine
I am at peace among the trees
Where I can feel this cooling breeze.

Alone again as evening draws to close,
It's morning now, and everything is dark
The still breeze whispers sweet nothings
In my ear, "Immortal love once again is true."
These years without her seem the same again
I am relaxed to hear her love for me
Was true. By the freshwater pond where
Life began I sit to contemplate the future;
The birds of the meadow sing the coming
Of another day at dawn, and to another
Dusk will this dawning day come. I've
Many years to live what will they bring?
Eternal love to heart is all I feel.

LAME REASONING

Lame reasoning laments these toneless ways
The trees weep fallen leaves these autumn days
Snowflakes turn to teardrops in my hazy eyes,
A cast of shadows turns hip friends into the dusty night.
Grip is in the air, the moonlight splashes
On the sponge painted canvas of the sky.
Final words are in the moody afternoon
With those little blue pills I see in the air,
How wonderful it is to be by her side
Her beauty outshines the sun on high.

Across the verdant verdure and her green
Columns Doric in their white splendor tower
Up across the frieze with Artemis and Pan
Or whatever his name might be gods all
Grecian to the core a pledge might say
No Spartan in sight to even the score
Open the roof where crows nest please
Where often they sit enjoying a breeze
With houses on Olympus or the Acropolis
They sent you up a retinue of Greeks
Back at the Bodensee, Arcady, or Araby.

COLLEGE TIMES

COLLEGE TIMES

A quiet evening at college
The lights turned down low
As a candle glows
Across this ivy campus,
And down below
In the streets of the borough
It snows.

When I think of her
With beauty seeming sweet
I thought she was real neat
How was I to know
Her passion was skin deep?
She always was so true
In friendship that arose
Like philosophers who pose
Questions of virtue or advice.
I thought she was so nice
Like readers who once chose
Thoughts above
Wine and love.

Out in the fields
On a frigid night
I drive alone
Lost on the road
In blizzards and wind
When memories begin

With loud music from the car
Out looking for a bar
To drown my sorrows in a beer.
One hand on the wheel
Two thousand pounds of steel
Lead foot on the gas
Looking for a blast
With a hidden stash
Avoiding being smashed
For another hour
I still had the will power.

I came upon her door
One night in the dark
It was my finest hour
She did not let me down
The news spread like wildfire
She was quite a sight
She had alluring power
And to this day she was the best
Even after she had left
She haunted my emotions
It must have been those potions
Not sold on the corner
Near the border
Of her hometown
Where the thoughts were so profound.

It was worth the effort
My college education
Every penny of it
It was esoteric
What I studied was enteric
But what really was the best
Came after she undressed.

MEDITATIONS WITH THE UNIVERSAL SELF

A voice descended from the past
And spoke into my ear,
"Take a being whose eyes you like
And shelter her warmth with your own.
Forget the others you have seen
And make my house your home.
Forget these words that I have smote
Upon the blazon of your soul
And I will grant you happiness
On top of zealous weal."

Old iron of the mind, I will not
Bend what truth
You apprehend in the light
Of original sin.
"There is a body good as gold;
Take her now before too late
And marry her to stock the fold."

"May you be blessed with innocence
Of childhood bliss
In place of aged remembrance
Of my voice and what you heard;
Thereby prosper, entertained,
Not waiting for another day."
Patience is virtue some will say;

I offer mine to the ashes of St. Joan
Who passing once my way
Called out, "Patience is a stone,
My burden will weigh you down,
Forget me, or be a martyr to your dying day."

I am intelligence I cried;
I won't be fooled
By a beggar or a grin
Recollecting on original sin.
In a street or in the fold,
Memory will not relinquish
Hold of my hand
For another's will to lend
To me direction
Where St. Joan met her end.

Or to St. Peter or St. Paul
I state my case:
I knew you all
Before the Fall of Man,
Devotion to the natural wind
Locked in vessels
That cling to the ground;
Infants still
Counting the times
This pebble has come round.

Here I am, standing
In the flames with Joan.
I am not alone,
For the wood was once
My family,
But after sprouting wings
Their genes called
And they abandoned me.

Gift of understanding without reason
Vaporize my dreams
And bundle them all
In a little cloud
Shadowed by the moon
On a shimmering lake.
One more afternoon
Without the pitter-patter
Of a heart within her womb.

I stand perplexed.
I am cursed by your hex
Pinned on a doll
With my name
You framed from wax
For a special guest
You wished to please.

The ebb and flow of the
Universal tide in my veins
Begins to grow then wanes;
Laden with heroic images
I step towards your flame
Offering hope of heaven regained.

THE MARTYR AND THE PROPHET

"Live long and prosper," said
The martyr to the prophet
"Live softly, die hard," said
The prophet to the martyr.
The martyr looked at the prophet
For a moment and replied,
"All is as it has been."
The prophet responded, "All
Is as it will be." Again
The martyr spoke, "Now
Is the end which will
Remain unchanged."
The mantic prophet
Prophesied thus, "Now
Is the beginning of what
Has yet to come, now is
A moment's notice corked
In a bottle in the depth
Of a mindless sea washing
The vacant shore." Again,
The martyr pressing his point
Vocalized his opinion, "The
End of the beginning is
The beginning of the end."
"The beginning of the end
Is only the end of a new beginning,"

The prophet rebuffing the martyr,
And the martyr emphasized,
"All for a wish and nothing more."
"All for a wish and nothing more,"
And the martyr and the prophet
Reached a common ground.

THE MARRIAGE OF BLACK AND WHITE

I went to the marriage of Black and White
To offer the band of the bond of two souls
She made a profane gesture with angry delight,
And turned like the others to seek vain goals.

I wished our hands on the Bible to page
She chose a book from the shelf instead
With a vengeance to strike off my head
Then left in a comfortable rage.

Led by the fragrance sweet gardens had sent
Found I the path to devotion's hall
Not flowers there, but their perfumed scent
Dabbled all on some coarse weeds tall.

I went to the marriage of Evil and Right
To hear the notes of that bridal procession,
But greeted instead by a funeral dirge
For a little girl lost in the night.

I went to the marriage with hope anew
Born in the resurrection of Christ,
But I saw with aghast mere sand they threw,
And called me fool for still throwing rice.

I asked the priest, he said with remorse,
"Prayer is the best I can offer this day
No marriage of minds will end in divorce
No matter how many love shall betray."

WRITTEN IN MEMORY OF A LOST LOVE

A blank page here awaits my eye
And seeks for guidance my pen to glide
Across this page like flying eagles,
White of head with keenest sight
To see you sitting with a frown.

What else is there my eyes can see
In your heart where none can be?
Since it is here I cannot see
I cannot speak your heart to thee.
What more I have to say you ask?
Is disappointment in the host,
Who has another date to keep,
And what comes next I will not say,
For in that secret
Repression lay, a word with meaning
You might get if you weren't dreaming.

Dream on dream what do you mean
Her back to me is turned.
If to one eye her head is turned
Then know that she has lied.
This I say from knowledge deep
That has kissed my cheek where
You have not, and where
Her lips did part

A blemish on my face
Like yours they call smart,
And now it is your eyes I see
Staring at me angrily, without
Words as if to say, "How come
All of this you know and
Still can't get the host to go."
And now from your head
My mind withdraws
So many hopes, so many
Dreams, so many lives
To see you in your days
When you are old
With embers in the fire
Glowing with the rose of youth
Now white with ashen death.
From this end my heart burns
With the beauty of your youth
Wasting your time thinking of me
When you could the best poetry
Be reading by the fire in your den,
By the flame in your heart,
If you cannot see the rhyme,
Then, I must say that you are blind.
What irony is this that now I sense
In your eyes I see pensiveness.
If you say enough with cheap time
Then I say in your heart there is crime.
If you say riches, crimes, nickels, dimes,
Where is your heart, your soul,
But in the banks of memory
That pure thought has bid me speak
So that I may tell you it is the weak,
The meek, the staid who have need;
My head, my heart, my hand

I extend to you by the fingertip
Pointing like a fountain pen
Like the fountains of the earth
That men have dreamed,
Of imagery
That I have seen on walls.
If my words here do not paint
The walls of the room of your birth
Then I should fulfill your prophecy.
The whip of your whim
The will of your whisper
In the night air to
A being warm who was not there.
If by sheer feat of memory
I can paint for you these words:
I can see caves and buffalo,
And the thoughts they pose upon the
Walls are the thoughts in your heart.
For in our hearts as in souls
Engraved the image of one mind
The truth, the glory, and sublime.

The image from my mind I pull
Is vile filth and evil swill
Where you will be
If you do not listen to the wise in me.
The eye of the wise of the wily sort
Have seen your kind in their time,
They say, "A girl most ably wrought."
To her I say, "Do what you first thought."
First to think, last to forget
That's what it means to be wise to me.
Be wise to consider the thought
Be wise to follow your heart,
And not your head

Which knows not direction,
But must be led.
In what direction yours may lead
I beg you take my heed,
And go where the children are fed,
And if you say there's no connection,
Then, adrift is my mind in the sea;
When in sight an island peers,
And on an island pears we have,
Bon appetite! The pears we have are me,
And I tell you the images I draw
I draw for you and not for me.
What the world everywhere lacks
That's love for you and love for me,
But love for you aplenty bounds
In leaps and jeeps in everyone,
But in your heart the word is hun,
And after that nothing but mum.
I have the eye, you have the ear
Together in your heart no fear.
May music play in the distance,
May music play in the schoolyard,
May your music play in my tears,
May my music play in your heart.
May you see the brilliance burning
Brightly ever brightly in the night
Like fireworks at the Fourth of July,
And still you ever wonder why;
Why does an infant cry
For mother's milk in need?
And if you there the host have found,
I wish you three the same fertile ground.

Time to retire
Time to go fight the muck and the mire.

Time is the essence of desire,
Time and care the fire to build
To warm the bones of the ill,
Of empty souls their hearts to fill,
To mine the hearts of empty men
Hunger draws me to your side,
Hunger draws the orange peel skin
And bids me savor with a grin
The segment smiling over chin.
With lips wet I go to taste
And find me there a bowling pin,
Of which I thought in haste.
A shiny row so carefully fit
No craftsman could compare,
There from the surface shines the sun
In the eye of the morning gleam,
And the faint go not
Where the bold will dare
To beat a silent drum
And beat a silent drum I do
So that the deaf might hear,
And if by chance I waken you
From the edge of your deepest sleep
May you take the Shepard by his hand
And lead with grace his sheep.

From the edge of your hard seat
Where will you soft comfort seek?
I see you often with the meek,
I see you often run,
I see you often poke in jest,
I see you have no fun.

If I could but cast
A ring of ever fluxing gold

To bind the laces of my net
To catch silver fish in the sea,
And if you had my golden ring,
Then the silver fish would be me.
If you are at home at heart,
Then let me hear your voice sing
Of life long lived,
But longing still to give
Your heart to a ring.
Ring in my ears the bells of notes
That you have dreamed
And I will write you like a seer,
If you call I will answer
If you answer I will call,
But this question presupposes
You have any heart at all.

NARCISSIST

"Narcissist," read the sign,
"Do not touch,
It is priceless art,"
Said the prince,
It's an old rag
You silly goose.
"It is my heart,"
But in the mirrored pool
Only an echo
Of a female voice,
"Be a fool and always look in my direction,
Be a fool and always love your own reflection."
Be content with your own inaction,
Be content with only a reflection.
Be gone fools and rags
Goose go find a gander
Not one your own gender
The wisdom is Greek
Do not take the word
I thought just last week.

WALK

You said I made you laugh and gasp,
You said I made your heart beat fast.
But who was that hovering by your room?
Who were those people in the hall?
Who they were you said you did not know,
Some one came to the door,
I should have walked out right there.

Your lips are like rubies in the sun
I know when in hot pants you like to have fun.
Here I am thinking about you again
Wondering awhile about the times
When I was in your room talking to you
About your many friends, none of which I knew,
And sensing another man on your breath
I should have walked out right there.

The times we could have had together
Upon the nights up north
You called me on the phone so much
And drove me to my room one night
With a shower of pecks on the cheek
What cold, vain, fruitless things are these
That passed for generosities?
I walked out right there.

ASH

All these cold and lonely days rolling butt end
Over butt end that never end, over and over again
To the bitter end and then only the ashes are left,
Blown away by a windy storm cold and far
Until it comes, the storm, blow by blow
Away it goes all these teeth between, lip worn,
Angry lit ashlights and where they go from where
They came, tongue in cheek, windy night after
Windy night is where it goes and what is left
No one cares about nor where the wind may blow it next
Except if in someone's eye it gets
Then someone cries because it hurt
Before they even knew what it was, whence
It came to be this thing called pain.

Until when next on and on another pain came
And someone realized they couldn't see
Eye to eye anymore because of the ash
In the other one. Be it match lit
Lip torn in between looking filter tips
Flicking ash bits in each other's lids
Or just a match to light a cigarette!
Light to light, tip to tip, lip to lip
Heavy breathing until I'm hip
Footloose and fancy-free wherever
My eye will be will see between
The white and black, blue and red extremes.
Hot or cold, warm after warm

Until perhaps one day it dawns
Another day will make it all go away
So way to go if that's your way,
The way you want to go today
Go with it day after day what more
Can anyone say, if that's what
Your love means to you today.

And when what's next is left
To take away whatever's left instead
Of what was once your wish to be
Then unless taken away by some
Gust of wind from out of another one's
Direction, forward to two, what can
One do without another one in store for more?

What's more in store but one
You think will open every door
Most of which are much of the same
Time will to none other but that one
Which be the same after every time
And every other one the same is done.
One in the same ever again
Over and over time after time
Ends become beginnings because
Where there's no beginning there can never be an end.

Burn be to burn ashes all ashes
Are the same, one name or another,
A name remains the same unchanged
Over change better believe it when
You see it 'cause you've got to see it to believe!

PART II

One lead me on ever again always forever
Evermore, dawn into sun, sun into day, one
Light will never fade away everywhere
I go; everywhere I've been, if I am
The earth around me the moon spins,
But one sun is the center of us both
And when it is night though full as the moon
May be, I know every wisp is but a twist,
Every light the moon may cast
Is but a sole reflection of our solar past,
Stars there are and there will be
Who will forever stand over me
Sometimes dim and sometimes bright
But if they all together could band
They might seem as bright as one
Sole, solitary star our solar sun.

All in one light all things come and go.

One lead me on where I may go
This time or another time until
The time I'll be no more with one.
One comes to one when past is past
And all the other ones are gone at last
One will agree all is one with me.

One is my home, my home is one
Here I may live forever not alone

I've seen it come; I've seen it go
Love lives the strongest when we're young
You'll find it true I know you will
I know you well I feel you do
For you're the one who never goes away.

You two will take your seed
To unsown fields to find another
One and hope to make that couple three, agree?

And when the fields are fresh
And spring is young begun
The time is ripe to find a life
Husband or wife who'll be with you
Offspring or none to have
And to hold when age is old
And winters' snow has covered
What once was better bare.

Stick to the first or hold what's last
Or love what it was you went
Looking for in the first place
And be lost. Now you can
Try and you can try, but
You can't count two until
The number one is through.

PART III

Tooting on the car horn
Cranking tunes down the speedway
Wild, hot-blooded babes
Integrate in the rearview mirror
While on the backseat
Butt ashes and dingy dust
Blow out the window
On drafts, like that of untapped brew
A whiff of spring permeates the air
And unfastened long, forgetting
Hair flutters in a breeze
Brought on by the original pattern—the pattern
In the clouds, fleecy cotton balls.

Tripping amongst feigned motivations
Laughing just to feel like friends
Seeing yourself in the eyes of others
Not looking for the truth for fear
Of finding it. Not taking it for what it is
When accidentally stumbling over it.
Mistaking youthful energy and exuberance
For immaturity, mistaking objects of affection
And attention for a sea of plenty in a wasteland
Talking yourself out of an oasis on the rationale
It is only a mirage, and asking who the person is,
Answering your own question,
And then wondering, "Who am I?"
Then hearing another's voice in your eye.

Don't look over your shoulder
Because if you don't know for
Whom you are looking you are
Only denying your own self-identity.
The world is created only in your
Own terms and not as expressedly
Espoused under careful understudy.
Ad lib and extemporaneously
Unveil the hidden treasures
Of Imagination's cove
Before the bird flies the coop!

MATURITY

THE GHOST LAND

Part I After the Burial

It starts
When I come to visit with a rose
And eulogize at the funerary
Where I encounter a cenotaph,
A monument to those who lived and died
For whatever cause or creed
They did profess
With the right to speak
Without retribution
Across this land of hallowed earth
Born before my time or after it,
Thrown into this world
Without a silver spoon.

A potter's reward
Apropos of charnel courage
Visiting a loved one
Now interred with rosary
In centuries unmoving,
Inanimate, decaying,
Flesh torn from sinews,
Sinews torn from joints,
Joints torn from bones,
Bones torn from life,
Leaving only bones,

Resting,
Where stirs the spirits
I am calling,
"Who can resurrect the dead?"
To live again
With a life worth living
In spite of a cold and distant past.

When,
Unlike this macabre winter scene
When pleasure gave us satisfaction,
And when satisfaction was a pleasure
Where ghouls appear and vanish
In the midnight air like mist
In April, dreams of spirits also stir
Thoughts of frightful days haunted
By tales of evil circumstance
Waiting, waiting for a weakness.

Let us also hold a candle in the dark
For the aged and infirm of humankind
May this spring season be a little warmer
To greet the needs of unfortunates
With no reprisals or injury,
A man's secrets are his own
Pray, perhaps, that he is not alone.

Allow us now to supplicate
An end to violence
Lest we become its victims
(Friends or family)
It has not bucked the system
Or budged the rock of Sisyphus,
Adamantine, obdurate, unyielding

A symbol of man's history
Unrecorded with divine actions.

So,
Upon a forlorn road at dawn I travel
Among granite stones and sepulchers
To offer condolence and oblation.
May mausoleums open
May graves disinter their dead
May evil be no more a part
Of everyday existence
With spirits, sprites, and ghosts
Arising, to return from the incorporeal
To live again in little ghost towns
All with tidy streets spic and span
Clean as linen freshly washed,
Sweet as sake freshly warmed
With a nightlight burning in the window
With a firm bed and a soft pillow
Rest your heads oh generations
Someday you will return.

Part II Living Monuments

A warm afternoon in May
Thunder soon gathers,
And when rain falls
And when lightning strikes
Not once, but thrice
Remember,
It is a reminder
Of a time
Not all too long ago
Rebel hands of men

Conspired against the Rock
They chose to alter
The juggernaut of history
And failed.
So let the fate of the world
Fall on every man
Give peace its due
And Paradise too
Time is not to waste
To live is no disgrace.

Yet,
Spirits seem to be immigrating
To the soul of this open nation
As we meander in a quiet way
Down a sleepy village lane.

Dull from exhaustion the nighttime passes.

When dawn arrives we are awaken
Doughty but stiff from the tumid air,
In this invigorating morning
The warm sun shines on our lethargy
With grogginess we arise
Like we have slept ten thousand years.

Slowly we embellish our empathy.
Slowly we acquire our stamina.

We sally distant from our houses and apartments
Which often look so deserted
As if spirits come and go,
As a whirlwind blows leaves to and fro
We hide the rejuvenated
Amongst family, friends, and institutes.

These citizens
Lay somewhere seemingly in secret,
This small municipality receives
A cryptic message
From a mystic capital
I peer along the smooth roadway
Each turn another magic village
All some secret bungalows
Where it unusually appears
Only local emporiums are occupied
Here people are,
But driveways all are empty
Garage doors all shut down
Here spirits live clandestine
In this modern ghost town.

We jog up and down the street
Where lives a chipmunk at the corner
A squirrel in a maple tree
Within a townhouse locality,
A raccoon dines on dinner
Or birdfeed in a backyard
Another spirit free, the wildlife
Outnumbers people on the local realty,
Where realtors feast on closings
And homeowners rare
Relish values, while prospective
Buyers marvel that splendiferous
Neighborhoods stand vacant
In ghost land reverie
Of another dying breed.

Houses look like faces
Trees dancing in the wind
All is dark late at night

A few lights here and there
White or yellow colored
Sodium lamps,
Or some headlights blue.
Christmas still is glowing
Old spirits nothing new
The lights are all on timers
Everyone's in Florida
With its ghost towns too.

Icy winds breathe and bitter chills freeze
Love and friendship, but I appertain
Amicability will see me through
My ghost will get me home tonight
Plodding along a path in jest
I come alone to a vacant nest
Where the woodlands are now ending
For developers must win
Where birds no more fly high
And when the camera's zooming
In upon the ground
Another town expanding
In suburban sprawl
To satisfy the ghost land public
Generating profits most windfall.

So, send that spirit soaring
Born again, but not a slave
Return, I say, from the dead
With ancient magic to this day
May wrongdoing not befall you
May the way be clear for you to ride
A chariot of angels winging
A chorus of cherubs singing
To the Afterworld or Heaven;

The promise of eternal youth
Is hidden from our view
Who would say it is not true
These years of scrutiny.

While able of mind
Thoughts blow on the wind
Shaking the branches of knowledge
Back and forth, they
Blow from far away,
Legends of ancient civilizations
Long dead
Seem not
All to distant traveling
On the wind,
It was but a short time ago
I feel
That Rome did fall
Or Egypt reigned
So let me say I scrutinize
The truth
And everything I question
To myself
Where no other soul can see.

The grand picture show
Of life obscures
Our view of reality
Of family ties
As far away
As Heaven
And as long ago
As forever.

Part III On the Road to Heaven

So, you want to climb
The corporate ladder
Become a rich man
In a day,
Just remember who the boss is
And what he's got to say
You cannot buck the system
Cheat before you steal
There is no profit in the margin
Just bottom line sex appeal.
So, when the big time comes,
And he calls you on the phone
Just hope the gremlins
Do not get you;
Remember who's the big man
To offer you a spiel
Don't ever have a problem
No matter what the deal,
Of this I would not think twice
Nor bat an eye or two
I just hope you can get real
Because the contract's signed and sealed.

A thought passes in the night
A memory comes into sight—a bonfire
Burning
For a pep rally
Many years ago,
I think,
Flaming in those dark oak logs
Is a sacrifice to halt the march of time
When such meetings were commonplace

There was a lost message
In this residential section
Where memories learned to die
Or hide, here,
In what was then
Modern America.

Boarded windows
Vacant storefronts
Gas stations with no gas
Clearance sales
Empty office buildings
Out of business
Some are bankrupt
Some are spirits in the wind.

Computers are most popular
All across the worldwide web
The Internet controls the Market
With search engines and explorer.
Information flies
Like a bird or soaring plane
Chat rooms and dot coms
Cross oceans and continents,
The latest in ghost land technology,
It's become the new theology.

The silent spring has come
Local streets vacated
As nature bears her pall
On a deserted morning road
Just at daybreak
A sparrow and some crows
Pass by,

Inhabitants of this ghostly town
We few citizens call home.

All across the nation
The cheap price of liquor
Entices
Ghosts from ghost town
Homesteads
To travel to taverns
Where potable spirits star;
Those with aspirations entertain
Ambitious, brazen, bold ideas
About philosophies old and new
With wisdom from afar
Until this inebriated crew
Stands up,
And staggers from the bar.

Where often there is romance
When I am out at night
Where I had a good time
My dime now running low
Before disconnected
I would have just
Liked to have said
When I think of you
I imagine
You were there
At the sunrise
Of the first dawn.

Parking in the churchyard
One summer long ago
I thought about the causes
Of social breakdown

Under the warm air
In this suburban ghost town
Early in the darkness
A cool breeze sharpening
My senses:
Mind and speech
Into a quick wit
With a whip of my tongue
Lashing mendacity
And false camaraderie.

Licking the crimson
Red cheeks of apples
Out in the daylight air,
Loving the weather—a moment
Rare, a priceless gift,
Then later,
The piece de resistance.

She was so beautiful in living
With her laissez-faire attitude
Although a bit promiscuous
I was her chief dude
What few times it did last
In the ghost land forest
When I was young and steamy
It left me longing and jealous
All those years I was alone
I tried public television,
Radio, VCR's, computer games,
Nothing was like her love,
I was miserable
Until I found myself
And the power I regained.
Someday

The pleasant times
Will return
Arriving in quiet lassitude
With friends
Inserting levity
To muse
About old stories,
And new.
'Til then,
I amass
A fortune
Of truth, wisdom, and knowledge,
In the latitudes of cold degrees
Harboring prestige,
Although in solitude
There is ice and snow
My heart warms to the presence
Of others.

Returning home
I end the night
Through the vacant streets
Through the empty years
Through the trepid tears
In this ghost land I come to my door
Destitute of lovers,
But full of words and flutters
Like birds in my heart
And feathers in my veins.

TAKE ME TO FOREVER

Take me to forever
In morning glory azure
I've missed three years tenure,
But time has proved better
Not waiting for another.

Take me to forever
Where you can't reach with a jet
Far from the rabble
'Til in heaven we have met
Not waiting for another.

Take me to forever
Ere another takes me over
With but this sky my only cover
With your blue eyes forever
Not waiting for another.

Take me to forever
For with me you'll never fret
My love lives forever
Because I never will forget
Not waiting for another.

Take me to forever
This link I'll never sever

Unbroken chain forever
Take me 'round with pleasure
Not waiting for another.

Take me to forever
And I mean eternity
Where the wind plays forever
To your raven melody
Not waiting for another.

Take me to forever
Where beauty's beautiful
Don't tell me maybe never
Just you and I together
Not waiting for another.

WHERE BENDS YOUR WAYS

Where bends your ways to your true love
Now I am gone my hand from glove?
Who mends thine heart once torn in twain?
Who cost thee tears now precious blame?
What voice you have my ears believe
Not what you say, but feel conceived;
Why is my love so ill received
When what you lost is not retrieved?
What's come to pass will not return
As we do live so must we learn
To live our loves and never spurn,
But make our peace or Heaven burn.

Where there is strife that broods to pain
Nowhere is need more visible
For sun to shine through too much rain
In answer to the miserable;
Nowhere is there an end too loose
To tie a knot, but in a noose
Around a neck for no good use,
Hang malice heart and not your ruth
As she who grants no suitor stay,
But sends her heart with hate away
To fancy him in Hell today,
Her love whom envy did betray.

COME HITHER

Come hither my love
And you shall see
Your true love
If I am he.

Go thither my love
And plenty you'll find
Who would enough
Fulfill your rhyme.

I trust my love
For you are bright
And hope your dove
Will once alight,

Come from above
Past storm or fright
To wish your love
A lovely night.

Where plays your love
In your dark head
Where stays your love
In these words read.

In peace my love
You may good find
If eyes my love
Were not so blind.

SHORELINE

O'er all the wild wastes of time, o'er all
The rough and ready roads, to the present
Have I come.

The monstrous rolls crest into waves
Crashing upon a clear and vacant shore.
Dawn breaks on the horizon and rises
A pale morning to a radiant day
As a blanket of fog lifts off the banks.

Along the strapping shore the pounding surf
In the elbow of Neptune's roar
Pestles the jagged rock and angular cliffs
To gentle powdered strands.

THAT GIRL THERE

The sun is shining in the sky so blue
On days like this I still think about you
So long ago it was you left my life
I'm sure by now you have become a wife.
I remember the day I let you go
It was so hard for me then to say no,
We kissed good night in a beautiful way
Now I think about you most every day,
Also, every month when the moon is full
How you swayed my attention with your pull
Of emotions and your desires strong.
The reason I left I tried to explain
With your great beauty I wished to remain,
But there were forces beyond my control
Throughout the years they have taken their toll
So if, perhaps, one day you read this poem
Remember that I wished for you alone.

SPLENDOR IN MY HEART-
PART I

I peer,
Across a homely tabletop
With worn-out veneer
Bereft of elegant enlightenment,
Absent in the opulence
Of understanding,
Mensal candelabra
Stands between us,
Unlit is the flame of inspiration.
Coldly the taper sits
With a wish
To be burning, burning
Ever brighter in our eyes
Surprised
To live our separate lives
Lying on the table
Pondering
If one of us will light the wick.

The full length of a mensch
With mirth
Seems to have followed me
From my birth.
A mirror in a window,
A mirror at the store
Reports back an image

That through the years
Wanders and wonders
In confluence of thought about how
We appear to others and how so much
Life reflects the better part of art.

A pretty face,
Rouge, mascara
Between our kisses
Eyeliner and shadow
Eying me out of the corner
Of her eye,
Playing mind games
Nearly insane,
In our heads and hearts
Considering important ideas
Versus one another
Wishing we could be
More than friends.

SPLENDOR IN MY HEART-
PART II

The style of a dancer,
Amid the grace of genteel tea,
And the charm of Casanova
Provokes the best in me
Who wishes now to rhyme
Like immortals through the ages
On all the silver pages
When upon the frieze I go
Like Orpheus, Sappho, or Ovid;
I hope I do not sound
Too pretentious or profound
With my college degree,
It cost me a real bundle
So please humor me.

The dawn is growing closer
The sky is cool and clear
Another day begins
With maudlin dew atop the winds.

The sun ignites
The morning
Burning ever blue;
Its crystalline gem
Empyrean hemisphere
Of light, cloudless;

Clear as a bell rung
In the distance
Playing the notes of sunrise
Which fade into sunshine
Aesthetic for the eyes.

The stars kiss daybreak
With pleasant good-byes
An airplane interrupts
The silence of amber thoughts
Evoked by viewing
A few joggers
And other passersby
Who concentrate on daily living
Conceived in media glitzes
Dedicated to meretricious fashions
Of maintaining healthy passions.

Young couples
Are like a new spring
With fish in the streams,
A child's dream,
Their faces beam.

The morning grows
With fiery grandeur
The yellow sun in concert
With the spirit of blithe flowers
Glowing in the garden
Like germaniums among the rocks
Or poinsettias in the hall
At home in the forum
I approach the door.

Into the thoroughfare

I trip, the hint of violets
In the air, the valor of their
Purple ardor under a heavenly
Dome. Lyrics hum along the roadside,
The orchestras of auto traffic
Buzz with our attention
As we hear songs from an album
Passing by with abandon.

As I leave for daily jaunting
I see, on the arm of an aiding
Waft of air, hungry
Bumblebees hurriedly
Wing for nature's nectar.

These medley days of summer
With water foaming on the beach
With swift familiar crescents
Of the waves washing children's feet;
Sandcastles fall to high tide
The moon is soon to rise
Looking for a good time
In a girl's eyes.

In the meaning of the waves
Of all the earthbound ways
Through many, many days
I have found nature lovely.
These times are precious moments
Enjoy each one as they come
The years will see no better
With each New Year begun
So take these words of wisdom
Find pleasure when you're young.

Multitudinous are the mountains,
Multitudinous are the seas,
Many years I've traveled
And many scenes beheld,
But beauty in her eyes
Made everything seem cold.

The eyes of you, the eyes of me
So often meet each other halfway
So be safe, so be secure,
But start to find
Your own dream
Do not let it slip away
Take full control
And find a way
To make your love
Come true today.

These college times
I find sublime
In these days told
Of how I'm bold
With women and with wine,
Now come with me, and you shall see
The secret of my art,
I write this speech
'Neath tree of beech
In the hours of the night
So come my way
We will some day
Alight
On a course
Of happy loving.

Now the bright noon
Takes love away
All too soon
When we are feeling
After our meeting
For others in their parley
That do allude
To such trysts
And dalliances moving;
I will approve
Your eyes of blue
The best in hearts
Is beating;
So come again
And be my friend
In this, and other
Callings.

Only to find a summer heat wave
Where some tan in UV rays
Others prefer the shades
Of a forest glade.

The brilliant day
Removes to eve
As I walk along
And wonder, I see
Pedestrians bound
For a carnival carousel
In this suburban realm
Giggling as they pass.
Shoots to blooms concur,
Annuals join perennials
Along the path
Maiden tulips and magnolia bells

In this mélange
Of summer's time-honored parade
Marching to the tempo
Of a mingled melody
Astounding still, yet filling
This serene concourse
With assonance and dissonance
Of mixed accord.

As evidenced by an out-of-tune piano
Somewhere punishing the breeze with discord.
I try hard to avoid the brutal,
Lugubrious, off-key sound,
But it follows me as I dash,
I feel out-of-kilter
As I see others,
Now in darkness
Talking, faintly, of love.
I am an unwilling audience
To him, that solitary player,
Hard pressed to find a living
Inside a once thriving homestead,
Sat upon his bench banging
Out notes. He flourishes
With inharmonious tones
As I flee his dirge-like clatter.

I travel down the road
Sirens, traffic, and horns
Merge together in cacophonous
Rhythms like a jazz band.
I happen on a building
Where I step inside;
Seats are carefully arranged
Around expensive tables

With soft, linen-like tops,
Pungent, appealing odors
Emanate from within,
I look at the guests,
My mind surges,
I forge ahead
Not waiting to take a drink.

I leave for better hours
Among streetlights and tall trees,
The night is warm and woozy,
Thunder strokes the air
We stop again for coffee,
A habit in this town
Bustling now with comfort
Like friendly faces in a dream.

A long draught of Turkish brew
Has taken an hour or two
Putting strength in my veins,
Youth upon my frame,
Hair dark as night
Tanned, olive skin
Dancing in the wind,
I thought,
Across this current city
Deserted like a barren gulch,
I would find myself here
Alone in early morn
No heavenly bodies
To greet me
With a cloudy sky above,
Quiet the radio,
Even the crickets are sleeping

No cars on the road
Silent in the darkness
Where thoughts are not too loud.

Radiant days of summer
Salubrious night of fitful slumber
Nine AM rolls round again
Repeating in diurnal
And nocturnal rhythms
The music of life.

SPLENDOR IN MY HEART-
PART III

Last eve a cool air
Blew through
Summer's scalding heat
Jostling healthy leaves
On trees
And flowers in the garden.

The swelter of August is broken;
It is now September and Labor Day.
On this holiday I stroll
Impoverished of emolument,
But plush in thought
As I ponder
An immense ostentatious living room
With a panoply of overstuffed,
Quilted sofas sitting unoccupied;
In the corner hovers a talisman
Foreboding apathy
And slothfulness
While we indulge our vanity
And gregarious feelings.
Women talk of hairstyles
Reading beauty magazines,
Here we cannot placate friends
When quiet music plays
With not a soul to hear it

In all the posh places
Popular people gather.

Pluvial precipitation
Pervades the environs
Winds note the end of summer
The equinox arrives
A few hot days left over
Remind us of the season past
Pools close,
The school year begins
Back in college
All is as it was before.

In the world of autumn
Long since the springtime thrush
Has called out in the evening
And made her nest of brush,
Autumn is the season
Of harvest and of thanks
The wry, crisp leaves of oaks
And maples emptied in the streets.
Remember, too, the mornings
Creep a little darker
As if the day were dying,
But nature does not falter
Nor ever give up hope
Of finding a new lover
When the first one did elope.

Whistling in the wind
On a brusque afternoon
The autumn leaves are gone
The church bells ring
Another year to bring

Cheer into our life
From coast to coast
From ocean to ocean
Across the waves and seas
Across the hills and fields
Where stands emotion
On a golden pedestal
Above all else.
Do yourself good,
Do not be dismayed,
Do not be distraught,
Find yourself a haven
Or a friend
Where you can have
Peace of mind.

I now end this literary junket
Traveling here and there around
The inner workings of a poet
Whose work will surely make a sound
Sweet and dulcet to the ear
With words in rhythms most prolific
In melodies and lyrics clear
That future ages find terrific
Come this fall and every year.

So let me say without a doubt
I hope to you my poem's sincere
On what life is all about,
Having brought along my gear:
A pen, a paper, and a lexicon
Versed in every ancient tongue
This poem is ending almost done
So let's conclude what was begun
With one short stanza more to hum,

Such music should be put to song,
And if it's not it won't be wrong
For me to stop before very long.

I think of all the times I've had
With ribald passion on my mind
And years of leers loose and profuse
With every profligate night of use
And every wanton, wasted day
With her the merry muse
Of all my lines and rhymes;
May they rise in times to come,
And chime in the listener's bell
For she the merry muse of writer's art
Is truly a splendor in my heart.

THE TEA PARTY

One sunny Friday afternoon in May
In 1898 or '99
A tea party so very fine
Was held in England near the Thames
The place settings were set in every detail
With lace doilies and linen napkins brand new
In a room you would soon agree
Was the stateliest tearoom in all the country
From Devonshire to the Hebrides
Done in grand and impressive style
With woodwork imported from Italy.
The attendants stoked the fire
To make the room warm and cozy.

Dame Edith was the hostess
Renowned for her hospitality,
Her attitude congenial
All in all most convivial,
Dame Edith was a dignified woman
A veritable paragon of society
In age somewhere around fortyish
Always prim and proper, strictly British
Having been schooled by all the best tutors
In etiquette and behavior,
She was born among the upper class
One step down from royalty
Her father had been a commoner

Who made his money
In the East India Company
For God and country
He lived well
He was knighted
Some years ago
For his service to the Queen,
As for his daughter Edith
She never had to dream
His property he did bequeatheth
To his daughter and to his son,
Dame Edith we have mentioned
Her brother Reginald
Now comes to our attention;
Having recently returned from India
Where he lived for seven years
Employed in the Exchequer
A government job without the fears
Of private business and bankruptcy,
A humorless man of sorts
With pince-nez, cuff links of ruby,
And chutney for his palate,
But always wise to money.
He was staying with the family
Expecting tea this afternoon
About four o'clock or so
With small talk and conversation
Religion and politics forbidden topics.
Dame Edith had a husband
Quite a man was he,
He was in the House of Commons
Elected quadrennially.
They lived here outside of London
In a house of Tudor design

By all standards almost a mansion
And never out of fashion.

It was approaching four now
The guests arrived punctually
If not punctiliously,
Exacting to a foible
Expecting tea enjoyable
At the four o'clock hour
Arriving comfortably
In horse and carriage
Most not being dour
Happy in marriage
Or engaged
To a fine, prosperous dandy
With anxious anticipation
Of the wedding day.
Having passed through the portcullis
Their banter, oh so gay
They stroll lightly across the patio
And on the portico they stay
Feeling very giddy
On this fresh springtime day,
It is a far cry from the city
With its sky dingy and gray.
Dame Edith was the hostess
Of whom all the servants boasted
Was the fairest in the Kingdom
For meticulous decorum
From China back to London
From Hong Kong to Cornwall
Her name was often mentioned
For hosting rich and famous
And guests of nobility too,
But Dame Edith was quite honest

About her upbringing and her station
She had a word for everybody
Compliments stated eloquently,
Sometimes even for her maid
When she stooped to bathe her feet,
Her voice rather melodious
Always sounding sweet.
But let us not digress
In our discussion hither
Our tea party yet to begin
With all its guests
Still left thither.

Dame Sarah first upon the porch
Not as old as you may think
A somewhat haughty disposition
Is how she appeared to many,
Her fashions though were funny,
But they would not say that to her face
Her dress subdued demurely
With bustle, shawl, and bodice.
Mrs. Starch was next to mount the stairs
A woman just past thirty
Whose passion was of fashion
She wore dresses of expensive cotton
Purchased in Paris or Marseille
With floppy hats
And décolleté and ankle length
Hemlines all white or beige;
She planned to visit the Exposition
Her traveling never seemed an imposition.
Ruth a girl of twenty
Lived in the same town
She was a volunteer
In a well-known charity

She was highly educated
And spoke with utmost clarity
Appareled in a corset and bonnet
Her figure stood out modestly,
Her father of some wealth
Sent her to the best of schools
By all rights she was pretty
The fancy of many men
As well as her fiancé
Of whom we will hear shortly.
Ma'am Muppet was a dowager
With a tinge of capricious character
And Dame Edith's children's nanny
Now a school marm by profession
That is when boarding school is in session,
And when it is not, a grand traveler
Always with a bottle of Grand Marnier
With money her granddad left her
On the continent she would alight
Her bric-a-bracs from vacations
Quite a sight. She had toured France
Looking for romance,
But that seemed out of the question
In this Victorian era
Sitting in a cafe
'Til all hours of the night, anyway.
Miss Lady Jane Grace
The last arriving
Almost always seemed so late
Her father was a lord,
And he could well afford
A private stagecoach,
But she appeared in such a hurry
Wearing her diamond earrings
And favorite broach.

The ladies now entered in the foyer
Relieved of ermine coats and damask umbrellas
Speaking of grand balls and royal galas,
They knew Dame Edith
Would not let them down,
She would not disappoint them
Now that Lady Jane had come to town.
The shiny floor was ebony
The walls were all of cedar,
The ceiling done in inlay
The curtains, tapestries from Brittany
Across the hall were Persian rugs
And hanging portraits
Of her genealogy.
Dame Edith had taken great pains
To make this day a festive one
She came out to greet them
As any hostess should do
A hearty welcome for all the invited
Who were in anticipation
Of delicious teas and treats.
She led them to the tearoom
All spread on the tea poy
Everything placed in order
The finest teas and delectables
Of all assortments,
With orange pekoe and lapsang oolong,
Earl Grey, English breakfast tea,
Darjeeling, and chicory,
From the hills of greenest China
From the halls of Angara,
Some fields perhaps in Burma
Dried in Calcutta, India.
The earnest ladies feeling hungry

Sat most expectantly
On chairs of Chippendale;
At the table, Dame Edith
With all the amenities
Chose herself to pour the teas.
The tea service was sterling silver
Beneath a chandelier of leaden crystal
Lit by burning candles.
In the kitchen the teakettles whistled
The tea balls full of tea
Steeping in the steamy liquor
With a twist of lemon
All was as it should be,
Sugar from Jamaica
Was in lumps in the sugar bowl,
Cream was in the creamer,
Plates, cups, and saucers
On the poy,
A serving tray and teacart
Made the tea set complete in every part,
For this afternoon in springtime
Would remain in every heart
As the tea party of tea parties
In this age of Queen Victoria
Spanning two entire centuries
Perfect in every detail
Perfect in every way
Upon The tea board stood a tea cloth,
The tea all ready in decanters,
In baskets in array
Were tea biscuits, breads, and cakes
With petite fours, gateaux, crumpets,
And other dainties, pies, fruit tarts,
And more. They all began to teaing
Before the sun had set

Those appealing herbal elixirs
Smelled so heavenly,
Stimulating conversation
With piquant ebullience.
They sipped each and every mouthful,
And ate each and every morsel
As if in the presence of the Queen herself,
So polite the speech was
In every nuance of correctness,
As we listen along,
"How fast the tea clippers are these days,"
Remarked Miss Lady Jane, "My Darjeeling
Tastes so fresh as if it were picked yesterday."
"Our British Empire so accommodating
To our palate and décor, it is quite
A shame though our Prime Minister is such a bore."
They all looked at Ma'am Muppet, her words
Not apropos, I think she took the hint,
And did not speak another non sequitur
Or faux pas. They totaled up their teacups
In salutation to the throne,
And said they hoped the Queen
Lived in as comfortable a home.
Then, they teaed and teacaked
And spoke about their lives.
Ruth said, "My fiancé is twenty-five
Born in Brighton by the sea
His family is well off,
And he is stationed now in Hong Kong
A lieutenant in the army,
He will be home in two years
To make me his wedded wife
He is planning a career
In business, a banker like his father,
And he never drinks a beer."

She called his father debonair
With his ink, his pen, and blotter,
But he really was a blatherer,
And, of course, a codger.
Next, Dame Edith's brother Reginald
Appeared in tux and hat
A truant host at best,
But at least he was not fat;
He removed his white gloves
And his tall, silk stovepipe,
And sat down amongst the women
He could not pay attention
He seemed preoccupied
He never had a girlfriend
He appeared almost stupefied.
A bachelor at heart they thought,
Dame Sarah asked a question,
"Praytell Master Reginald
I hope you do not mind my asking,
But what is it that you do
Down in that jungle land you are living?"
"I work for the Exchequer,
But I am not in such good humor
As everyone can see
I am often at a loss for words
It is not my cup of tea."
At this all the ladies laughed,
And thought it a great joke
The pun though not intended
'Twas all that Reginald spoke.
They laughed some more
And passed out crumpets
And petite fours with tea
The time flew by like hours,
Mrs. Starch a quiet woman

Who before had not said much
Began with words about her father,
"He worked his fingers to the bone
Owning a shoe factory
'Til his hands looked tanned like leather,
He made pounds of money and gave
Me a huge dowry.
My brother he put up in business
Running the company,
My sister married wealthy,
I a solicitor
He won many cases
In jurisprudence law
He is working currently in London
Charging six pence or a crown."

"Remember," said Dame Sarah,
"We never speak of politics
Or religion for that matter.
So, if you mention the Black Hole
Of Calcutta or the Opium Wars,
Or the trouble with the Boer,
It would be most impolite,
Not with aplomb or discreteness,
Our hostess would not chide you
Her demeanor is so right
She never says she notices
Our foibles or our faults, however slight.
I hope I have not overstayed my welcome
It must be half past six,
I most graciously wish to thank you
For this afternoon's entertainment
I hope you enjoyed our company,
And invite us back again someday."
"Praytell, let us stay a little longer

The dainties are half eaten
And my dinner is still in the freezer,"
Quoth Ma'am Muppet one more time,
The doilies were not soiled
The linen napkins in their laps
Dame Edith's children are returning
From their school time afternoon naps;
Her husband Alfred
Is seen coming up the walk,
He enters by the front door
And responds, "Party is over ladies,
Time for solid food
Tea is fine and dandy
For the afternoon,
But beef in all our stomachs
Will put meat upon our bones,
A fact of which I am sure you are aware,
Taught to every youngster
In the British Isles
Since the age of ten or twelve.
So all you ladies find your drivers
Your coats, bonnets, and attires
Dinner is served at seven
Here at my happy home,
And I feel like I could masticate
A beef Wellington
Slapped onto my plate.
I am sure your party was tremendous
With spiced tea from the orient,
But it does not satisfy a hungry man
Unless he comes from Ghent."

Thus ends our grand tea party
The best in all the lands

They never saw a better
If they searched as far as Cannes
Maybe next year will bring another,
But considering the weather
And all the frivolous fun
The canorous light banter
Since the teaing had begun
It was the greatest tea party ever
The conversation so witty and so clever
This sublime tea party now over
Was the most superb of all time.

THESE TEARS (FOR YOU) OR THIS LITTLE BOX

Contained herein this little box
Are all the tears I've shed for thee
Sleep with them safe, close to your heart
Please do not open lest they escape
This little box special to you
And evaporate like the morning dew.
Don't cry for their loss with teardrops too
I'll give you some sol I know it's not much
If you can't have what another can do
I'll take your word I'm it to you
If you'll excuse how hard I cry,
I'm missing out, these tears for you.

I'm putting out my tears for you
It's not lend-lease, beg, borrow, or buy
It's just for love I know you do
I'm not asking much considering all
The things you have gifted to you
But these are yours I heard you say
Don't let another take them away
They can't replace but they can do
Your burning up what you once said
These tears put out, these tears for you.

LIBERTY BELL

In this frenetic frenzy rhymes the chimes
Of bells so fine.
Like a cherry flapping in the wind
The iron ball goes bong, bong, bong;
High atop the hallowed hall
The bell rings out, hearken to its call
The bell rings out in clean, strong
Notes, like a musician's
Magic tone, bong, bong, bong.
So long ago, but not today, when that bell
Did loudly play
Bong, bong, bong, on that first Independence Day.

Proud, stern pronouncements
Loud and clear, throughout the town
For all to hear, the people wake
To sound the notes of freedom's call
With arms and revolution.

Through all the years
And all the fears
Of populace in redcoats' face
The bell rang out in peaceful grace
And pied parade
The coming of a new country
Conceived in rights inalienable
And versed in true democracy.
So when the years go passing by,

And you argue with the government
Remember America's the best there is
With its standard born in equality
That fought against tyranny
For that sweet girl, Miss Liberty.

And with her bell, broken now
The years will garner memories
Like legends of the ancient past
Of how men fought and how men won
The right to celebrate
On Independence Day.

Bong, bong, bong.

WHEN THE SONGBIRD SINGS

Lonely evergreens stand
Deep on a woodland hill
Pine needle bed beneath
Crystal lakes nearby,
An undergrowth of brambles
Where blueberry bushes
Look like neon lights,
In a thicket deer are blended
Against a background of green leaves
Melting in summer heat;
I can hear the forest's breath
As trees speak through the breeze,
I see a rabbit flash
In the twinkle of an eye
On trails not often trodden
In the walks of a passerby;
Laughing flowers smile
The wooded floor is liquid
When rain begins to pour
The sky is dappled gray
On this weekend out of doors
With nature on display;
So many ways my life
Has turned,
So many times the earth
Has turned,
But still I love the woods
When the songbird sings.

BIRTHDAY SONG

Dear Mom,

Another year has flown
Under your protective wing
With strength and motherly love
And the good things that you bring
Into my life a cut above
What others sing,
Thus on your birthday I write this song
Because in mine eyes you can do no wrong.

FATHER'S DAY

On this day I'd like to say
To you my dear swell dad
Through all the years
You worked so hard
You never did seem sad
So when this day
Comes every year
And you receive this card
I hope it makes you glad
To be my dear swell dad.

This special day again is here
To give thanks to you and fathers everywhere
For all they do throughout the year
Making their families happy, wealthy, and wise.
So sit back and enjoy a moment or two
Before you have something else to do
On this Father's Day.

Have a happy Father's Day
For all that you have done
You've fought so many battles for me
And I'm glad that you have won
It's an uphill fight in this world
And many here have faltered
But you keep pressing onward

Until fallen is the foe
So onward press undaunted
And lay my critics low.

PEOPLE I HAVE KNOWN

CHERYL

Your happy face and cheery smile
Always brightens our day,
Your vivacious and ebullient personality
Brings joy and gladness to our hearts,
Your friendliness is a pleasure to behold,
A calming respite in this world so cold.

And when we come seeking guidance
You always lend a helping hand
In matters great and small.

So, Cheryl, take a bow for us
You've grown quickly to become a trusted friend
In all you say and do,
You've really made a lasting impression
Since you have touched our lives.

We hope you will be with us
A long time in the future
With all the positive attributes you feature.

TO MY DEAR VERA

I stood like a statue before the temple
Of your figure
Full of love and full of vigor,

Thinking of you
My honeydew,

Shorn in forest green,

Bathed in the light of morn,

Together in a field
Loving you like loving nature,

Seeing you a sight to see
Like an angel heavenly,

We are fish
Who swim in the same
School,

Eying you
When first I saw
Your brown eyes so cool,

Your flashy locks
Your visage stocks
In store for me,

Roll back your head
When we are led
Together in the night,

Lonely as a star at dawn
All night long, o'ershadowed
By the mysterious light
Of the setting silver moon,

A murmuring spring
Chortles in the dark
As I toss and turn to sleep
Thinking of you deep,

The sun arising in the east
Without sleep, without sleep
A hearty breakfast to eat
Without you, without you
So neat.

JOANN'S PLACE

A quiet retreat amid the hubbub of suburbia
Our old friendly clique listens to the stereo,
And watches television while our conversation
Drifts from one pleasant idea to another;
We talk about past and common interests,
We laugh a lot and smile at situations
We were in that once seemed gloomy,
But now they all seem so groovy
Here at JoAnn's place.

The furniture is antique and we are all in the pink
We all feel well as if we were in some forest dell
We all have expensive coffee, and sometimes order pizza
Chinese food a great mainstay, we always have a great time
People, places, things that got us down now appear
In a different light on the outskirts of town
Here at JoAnn's place.

With the air-conditioning on all summer
We are cool and comfortable
With tender lighting and a pretty picture
On the wall, JoAnn is always kind and cordial
We enjoy her honest candor, she is happy
To have her place far from the maddening crowd,
With Cheryl her friend from downstairs
They are quite a pair, cracking jokes about society,
And the work force, common themes among our dreams
Here at JoAnn's place.

So all in all we have to say this is the place to stay
When you are feeling blue, when you feel you have nothing to do
Just go see JoAnn and she'll cheer you up,
She'll tell you what a good friend you are,
And all about her getting a used car,
With her friendly and jovial character
She really has such great charisma
She made it far in the business world,
And has seen many companies fold,
But somehow she has made it through
To own a marvelous condominium here,
Here at JoAnn's place.

So if you come to call on her
Remember to bring a fancy coffee
She never goes to a bar,
Don't think to meet her type there
She is more sophisticated by far,
So when you think of JoAnn's place
Remember it's a haven
For many heartbroken souls,
They come and go around the clock,
And they always get good advice,
And JoAnn is always in a friendly mood,
And do her a favor, bring some food,
And you as well as us can have a good time
Here at JoAnn's place.

DEBBIE

Debbie with a heart
As big as the moon
She ingratiates herself to us
With warm friendship and humorous conversation.
A stiff critic,
But with a personable disposition
Always a stickler for excellence
She never settles for second best.
In her mind there must be
Many thoughts of love and joy
To help us through hard days
When we try to cope with problems
Both big and small.
Laughter within her often
Bursts forth upon hearing a funny joke.
With her favorite lines
From poetry and jocund vignettes
She has artistic character
Very jovial and Jovian.
Not impressed with words
Too big to understand,
She always has something to say
Between her Avon and Lifesavers
A Tums or two with eyes of blue.
Always supportive and good natured
She really makes my day

When she blows me a kiss
In the wind on our way
For coffee in the morning
On the Starbuck's Express-o.

MORAL ON A MONDAY MORN

If you come by me a calling
With a man around your shoulder
I won't be there to fain a blessing
On an illegitimate foundling;
Though your favors I have tried
And found them to my liking
I will let them pass and slide
If you dishonor and besmirch my pride
Neither for remembrance sake
Or a promise never asked
Will I ever stoop to hate
But make no mistake
My aim is to possess
A being sought out from the rest
Who is wrought among the best.

By my side or by another
Pass your time unlike a bride,
Unlike a bride that broods
Around a groom. Canter all around
The town to the cast I am no use
I will fast and groom my bride,
There is feast where famine died,
To the claim you do not know me
A feast of sighs a sight for sorry eyes.

I will not have a lady friend
Who struts around with other men,

And worships truth before my eyes:
Who offer tooth and nail a gem
And worships tooth and nail a jewel
And not the truth like honest fools.
I have seen enough to know
Your heart at best and heard
To sense you have a heart
Of little faith in earnest men.

My dreams instead
You cast about
While you profess abstention
I listen not,
But read your grin
Which tells it like it is
A pretty lady a bit
Uncouth about her ways
Of jade. Diamond of hope
A promise too; take me,
My gem of priceless pearl.

Take me prize or leave
Me the prize of an oyster shell
Lean upon another's faults
Smile on the facet's gleam
All crowns of this world
Are false, salvation does not
Depend on you
Enlightened enough to
Need no crutch.

TO KATE

When you're feeling down and lonely
And you're heart is sinking low,
Remember there are many
Who feel the same way too.

And if the world seems most uncaring
And not a friend that's true,
Remember there are many
Who need a friend like you.

And if your life seems lacking
In things that you do need,
Remember there are many
Who have more need than you.

And if there still are those
Things you cannot do,
Remember there are many
Who will help you to shine through.

And if there still are those
Who want you doing
Things you don't want to do,
Remember there are many
Who will stand by you.

So, if the world seems hard and biting
With no success in store for you,

Remember there are many
Who will still remember you.

And if you feel at times
Your life's not going well,
Remember more than just your friends
Wish you are feeling swell.

If it seems your problems grow and grow,
Remember all of those
Who have learned to take things slow
Hoping life turns out a rose.

And if there is no solace
In anything you do,
Remember to have patience
With those who feel as you.

Hoping you feel better
In the times to come,
Wishing the world were fairer
Than what to you it's done.

So may my pen rest easy
With this poem composed,
And may your eyes be happy
When in books these words repose.

POEM TO JENNY

It is true a mountain is a beauty mark
On the face of the earth,
True sheets of rain fall on the bed
Of the brokenhearted,
True a blanket of snow covers
Mother Nature's winter sleep,
True a carpet of green grass comforts
A virgin flower,
True the eyes of the forest watch
A branch of knowledge grow,
It is true the fire of eternal life
Burns in the ichor of God's veins,
May He give His torch to you
Carry its fame forever true.

It is true the fruits of passion
Will bear a child of love,
True the mouth of mankind
Thirsts for the fountain of youth,
True love is food for thought,
True the sands of time
Will bury a corpse of lies,
True the winds of fortune
Will uncover the secrets of time,
True the works of man
Are transient in the eyes of God,
True the works of God
Seem strange in the eyes of man,

True a flood of news
Can alter the course of the river
Of history,
True unrequited love
Can fade in another's arms,
True pleasures of the flesh
Really blow your mind,
True love is blind,
True love of sex
Prefers not a permanent nest,
True a pretty face
Can turn a head,
True fame and fortune
Can lead to early death,
It is true calling birds sing
And church bells ring
For the coming of the Lord,
And the redemption He will bring.

It is true the fate of man
Is not in his own hands,
True the hands of fate
Control the destiny of man,
True the hands of time
Turn on the clock of eternity,
True the face of time
Stares at immortality,
True a lover's gaze
Longs for a perfect face,
True philosophy
Reflects in the mirror of reality,
True a woman's face
Is the epitome of attractiveness,
True the passage of time
Leads to the roads of Heaven,

True a point of understanding
Exists on a line of reasoning,
True a spark of inspiration
Is kindled by creativity,
True the fish of the sea
Swim in schools for company,
True the door to enlightenment
Swings on the hinges of faith,
It is true the house of the Lord
Has foundation in our souls.

It is true the leaders of mankind
Lend themselves to the banks
Of popularity,
True the influence of ambition
Corrupts the mettle of integrity,
True your journey through life
Will bring you to self-identity,
True the reign of emperors
Pours tyranny across the land,
True heads of state
Make deals in smoke-filled rooms,
True a good country
Is where freedom starts,
True years of dissipation
Can drive you to the end
Of a one-way street,
True years of dissolution
Can drive you to the end
Of the road of life,
True time can recover the rocket
Of earlier launches in life,
True the scales of justice
Weigh in favor of the innocent,
True truth comes

From the mouths of babes,
True good things grow
In the garden of charity,
True a good start
Is a road to the future,
True chastity
Befits the young,
True a spectrum
Of the human condition
Is like a rainbow in the sky,
True love can lead to happiness,
True happiness takes wing
When your bird of paradise flies away,
True years of hardship
Can make a man callous,
True the love of women
Can be both a blessing and a curse,
True a wave on emotion's ocean
Can raise the depth of contentment,
True the mask of an honest face
Can disguise a crooked heart,
True the sky is the limit
When two lovebirds take flight,
True years of indifference
Can paint a different picture
On a model of objectivity,
True years of neglect
Can rust the engine
Of your mind,
It is true that God is good.

It is true a stranger's eyes
Are windows on his soul,
True a poor man's labor
Will gain reward in Heaven,

-HERM

True the bluebird of happiness
Will return after an angry storm
Of jealousy,
True seeing is believing,
True years of happiness
Can end in divorce,
True love
Can end in disaster,
True love
May never end,
True a stitch in time
Saves nine,
True streams of the dreams
Of youth run wild and free,
True the murmuring brook
Speaks with the voice of nature,
True the wind
Blows a girl's hair
And makes it more beautiful,
True a beautiful face
Can define an age,
True the heart of man
Beats for the approval
Of a woman,
True, "It is easier for a camel
To pass through the eye of a needle
Than for a rich man to enter
The Kingdom of Heaven,"
It is true the Lord is with us
Even when we are alone.

It is true a friend is true
Who treats you right
And does not leave you
Feeling blue,

True a friend is right
Who gives you good advice
And does not steer you wrong,
True a friend is a friend
Who does not make demands,
True a friend is good
Who understands and offers
To lend a helping hand,
True friendship is found
If like a tree it grows,
True a friend is proud
If he is proud to be
Your friend,
True friendliness
Will last if the person
Writes or calls,
True the rose
Of friendship grows
From virtuous deeds,
True love flourishes
In a forest of pleasure,
True a state of bliss
Exists in the meeting of two souls,
True vows of constancy
Make the flower of love last,
True the heart in time
Beats for peace of mind,
It is true the days of our lives
Are numbered by God.

It is true you have found a friend
When they kiss you first,
True the seeds of friendship
Grow on fields
Of mutual reward,

True the flower of youth
Grows better in a warm
Emotional climate,
True the buds of love
Blossom better
Without a rain of tears,
True a friend
Will be with you in the end
If his heart is with the Lord,
True the Lord is good
And capacious of heart
For he will save your soul
Where another man will not,
True Jesus is your friend,
It is true death is not always
Forever.

LOOK BEFORE YOU LEAP

Look before you leap
Stay not too long asleep
The rude awakening for some
Never seems to hide
The sun from out the sky.
The day midmorning still
The dew is long and dried
On the walk a strolling few
Who talk of jest and fun
But are sure to lend a hand
In the event of a hit-and-run.
My fate once great and grand
In all I do or do not understand
Is sealed to last until,
The last ration of my can is tinned
My glass is cracked, unspilled
Not for want of sand or thrill.

Wishes once were young
Those that live them down
Those that live them up
End always in the ground
Where once it all began.

Don't believe there is a ghost
That leads me right
When I am lost.
Believe there is no bright

That beacons through the dark.
Believe not that there
Is right and false
But that a man
Must have two hands
Before the first is lost.
I prophesy the worst
But live to kiss
You all good night.

And be wise not to hurry
Lest you forget the best as blurry.
God and sun, mother country
Make the best of what you can
Like all the rest since time began.

Achieve it all, possess it none
You can't return what you've begun
Without regrets or pride, or hate.
Someday maybe we'll be great
I have no care but that if we
Ever part we may part as friends
Under one that all may love
The olive branch, the mourning dove
That to me is God enough
That I may lead the lack
That others follow.

I can count unbiasedly
And that is all
Without thought to attitude,
But not to bore with platitudes,
Sandy,
I would be a fool
To ever be sore at you

Still I'm mad when you treat me poor
And for all you're worth
I will not stand
To see you with another man
When I am there to take your hand,
But curse
And live on from there
And rather stand and curse some more
I'll just claim no understand
And offer up another soul to blame
This is you I do attest
For if it were me I would
Not worry, but only try my best.

Make your mind of one no more
Only there is peace at heart
I claim no rule of witnessed law
For what is truth cannot be found
And the more one looks
The more the breath of Him withdraws,
But still be sure to look around
And still be smart if not profound
The more you fret on what is sound
More faults you'll find,
But no renowned,
Listen first to learn
With a vow n'er to spurn
What you may find,
But take it in and make it home.
I know you and you know me
Whether you do or not agree
We once were one, then two, then three.

That's why I don't drink gin
Among other reasons, all that trim

If you can't make head or tail
Begin,
Because what good girls want is really sin.
Take it fast or make it last
Give it in God's name or none
Don't let guilt spoil your fun
Because your spool will once be spun
Don't count on worth to make a bank
Out of someone else's loss.
All else is said, all else is gloss
Though blessed it stank
And so it sunk
For want of you to rescue it
And what it was I will not say
Though I am sure it liked to stay
Don't take life for granted, girl,
You're good enough for any's wife
If my words have found me right
In the judgment of your might
Let me add, don't you be mad
If you found truth you should be glad
To follow suit and not a fad.

So before I find another rhyme
Lets you and I together find
A time together with one mind.
Take care your physic good to keep
Not like me or some low creep
Take care a body does remind
To keep your health
Lest I go blind
Or no one else is there in time
The hint is veiled, the crime unfurled
In your girl grin I see a sin.

My heart is still another place
That's not to say you're not real nice
That's not to say you wouldn't do
Or that I wouldn't live with you
With yes and no my choice
But only that my heart is true
Enough to confide in you
Love that's true is mute of voice
Take my word of God's advice
Go to the first you wanted to.
The rite is but a symbol, girl.
Don't believe I have seen the light
There is the spirit of the Ghost
That Christ the host was body to.
Though this song out time may last
What's first is first will never pass.

LOOK BEFORE YOU LEAP
(REVISITED)

There is sense and there is nonsense
And of these two, nonsense is stone blind.

Bone of contentious argument
Beats the drum of psychic armament
While the circus' center ring
Revolves about the sun
Revenge is still no fun
No matter what each New Year brings.

Jealous envy:
Love that lasts for money
Is love of money
Without the gift of worth.

Burnt to a frazzle
Fried to a crisp
All for a tassel
And a mortarboard tip.
All that is, all that is not
A man's soul is a woman
A woman's soul is known
Only as a world of knowledge and a fast town.

Desire me not
Take another to wed in your heart.

Desire one not
Take another to wed
In your heart
As well as your bed.

Not one desire hot
To make love
In your heart
As well as your head?

Hotheaded hostility
Masks a passionate heart
Threats are futility
If love there is not.

Flower of a face
Wed to fertility
Grant a man grace
In place of eternity.

Sword in a stone,
But one can remove
Needle in a haystack
Cannot be removed
But by one whose youth is unmoved.

By one,
By one girl alone
Whose youth is unused,
Bone of contentious armament
Pierce another's argument
Before the last is known
Before the past is gone.

Dark eyes of invention

Brown with cool lies
Green curiosity cries
An ounce of retention
For a pound of good-byes.

Cruel means of abstention
Belie a crude need
In envious greed
Of influenced persuasion
For instilment with seed.

Bombastic diatribe
Pierces the night.

Sparkling teeth,
Glistening ruby lips,
Cup my palms around her cheeks
And give this sweet rose a kiss!

Take her hand
In step to dance
And let the band
Keep to the beat.

What has been time is time again
Fed out to the endless end
In borrowed measures, sifts of sand,
Collected in gutters, stranding the streets
Eroded blocks of granite
Chiseled from the planet
To shield the seed of chance's toy
And plant the tree of gracious joy.

Come one, come all
Come once for one

Before the fall
Come many in one
Come one in many
Come all for plenty
All for one
And one for all
All at once
Once and for all.

ROZ

Oh, girl you seem so serene as can be
You so pretty and nice with to be
You have such style, you have such grace,
But what I like about you most is your face.
So please to pleasure me with your presence
Come with me and we'll go to a dance
On midsummer's eve in the middle of France,
And I will try to act really friendly
Before the party gets real tawdry.
These years since I have known you well
Really freed me when I was trapped in Hell,
They seemed like eons of forever,
But with you here life is better,
We'll bring along all our buddies;
Sheila, Debbie, Paul, and the downtown crew,
But remember I really think of you.
You're just great in everything you do
Even though some people think we're nuts
I consider you someone I can trust.

THE M-MAN

So you really are the M-Man
And you really are from E-Land
Isn't that marvelous, isn't that grand,
We can't say what it stands for,
We can't say where it is
Don't ask me any questions, I won't say any more
Except to say a little
In a riddle just like this:
It almost rhymes with funny,
And sounds a bit like dummy.
It's cool to be the M-Man
When no one knows your name
It's cool to be from E-Land
Of grand and classic fame,
So if you meet the M-Man
Just passing on the street
Remember he's from E-Land
A place that can't be beat.

A MAN AND HIS WINK

Once there was a man who winked
With a twinkle in his eye and knowing smile
And some would say he never blinked
But they all knew his cunning guile.
All alone behind his eyes soul searching
He sat among his friends and looked
Stylish and handsome with smart talking,
Just enough to get anyone hooked,
And with his penetrating eyes there was that wink
Though often they said his confidence was waning
It was enough to make you think
How easy it was for him not to be straining.

Oh, how the girls swooned for him
His wicked face and confident wink
That made the girls love his every limb
And in their minds he really made them think
He was the greatest thing since Casanova.
All because of his sexy wink
All the girls became his pushover
Maybe with a flower or a kiss he'd slink,
He was as lucky as a four-leaf clover
Statuesque he stood, he did not blink
He soon made every girl his lover
All in the wink of an eye forever.

SONNET INSPIRED BY JANET

Immortalize forever on this page
Your snowdrop hair and blue bejeweled eyes
Graceful beauty in this or any age
With sapphire skin and virtuous guise
That glitters on thy smiling lovely face
Thy blushing love and passion of the heart
Bearing renowned in this or any place,
In eternity deemed a work of art.
With thumping ardor of thy suitors' will
Eligibles so often come and go,
But you are the master of your sweet fill
And keep your sweetest favors still in tow:
A flower fresher than the rose of youth
Here in verse your memory and your truth.

INSPIRED BY JANET

May peace be with you every day
May your tree of life never sway
May your fragile heart never break,
And may fine potions your desire slake,
Though years come and years go
May your lover never say no
So seek harmony where you bend,
And your detractors never apprehend
Your secret garden far from here
In your mind, your thoughts there;
And in peace, love, and happiness
The world with your endeavors impressed,
With all the virtues you are blessed.

TO _____

I have seen life's greatest chances
Slip away with the rising tide,
I have seen swift fleeting glances
Dream for a brighter side,
I have seen the solstice zenith
Is no solace when eclipsed,
I have seen the soul of sorrow
Drown in acrimonious lips,
I have seen the best fall fallow
As impudent acerbates,
I have seen the deep and shallow
Purloin another's breath,
I have seen robust and callow
Shirk grace where all is blessed,
Contemning past experience
In fearfully facing tomorrow's rest.

-HERM

SWEET WONDERFUL SUE

Sweet wonderful Sue, I think of you
Whether you are near or far away
When others hear this song they'll love too
The way you look and persevere through
Persevere through, persevere through, persevere through...

And when adversity strikes
Your beauty shall shine through
Shine through, shine through, shine through...

Every day I think of you
Much to my distraction,
If you find me an attraction
I hope you follow through
Follow through, follow through, follow through...

We all have our days,
We all have our ways
It seems changes I've been going through
Going through, going through, going through...

And after the changes
I hope one thing will come true
That we'll never be through
Never be through, never be through, never be through...

Because I love you
Love you, love you, love you.

OH BONNIE SUE

Oh bonnie Sue with eyes of blue
Of you I have been dreaming
Oh bonnie Sue with eyes of blue
Your face is always beaming.

Oh bonnie Sue with hair of gold
So many have been bitten
Oh bonnie Sue with hair of gold
Of your beauty it is written.

Oh bonnie Sue your figure full
Your spirit is indomitable
Oh bonnie Sue your figure full
Is so lithe and lovable.

Oh bonnie Sue the sight of you
Makes my heart go pitter-patter
Oh bonnie Sue the sight of you
So many want to flatter.

Oh bonnie Sue your love so true
Smitten with a feather
Oh bonnie Sue your love so true
For me there is no better.

Oh bonnie Sue knowing you
Will not be with another

Oh bonnie Sue knowing you
For me there is no other.

Oh bonnie Sue my love for you
Never will be waning
Oh bonnie Sue my love for you
Will always be a-longing.

Oh bonnie Sue so warm of heart
Throughout the years I think of you
Oh bonnie Sue so warm of heart
Your faithfulness in love is true.

Oh bonnie Sue so far away
Over hill and dale together
Oh bonnie Sue so far away
I'll think of you forever.

Oh bonnie Sue I will love you
Through days of honest toil
Oh bonnie Sue I will love you
But with jealousy I boil.

THE PASSING YEARS

When I think back
On the good times
I had, there are
Many that cross
In my mind,
But when I think
Of you my sweet
A tear comes
To my eye
Thinking that
Somehow you
Were left
By the riverside
When the
Pleasure boat
Of life embarked
And though I am
Sure there are
Others who missed
The boat as you did
My attention turns
To you,
Because you always
Held a special place
In my heart
Since you were beautiful,
And beauty always was
Special to me.

MY PEACE

My life has been a struggle
You are my solace and respite
Through great burdens of confusion
You give me the gift of understanding.
In the hubbub and the hustle and bustle
Of the fast paced world
You have quiet consideration
For all those things
That appear a challenge.
With you I feel the comfort
Of a lover and a woman's touch
And through all my life of faults
You are my saving grace,
My whole existence once seemed a war
And now you are my peace.

PHILOSOPHIES AND NATURE

WHERE IT ALL BEGAN

The humble lark and pied peacock
Alone in this shady, quiet bower
Green with spring where saplings rush to grow
High as the old oak trees and conifers
High as the evasive fog that lays upon the treetops
There is a robin redbreast calling,
The first this year I have seen, skittering
In and out of a bush as it plies
A worm from a grassy nook, a gaggle
Of geese sojourns near a lily pond,
A flicker hops on a solitary path
Then disappears under a thicket of brush
While a sprinkle of dew bedabbles the dawn,
Glistening in the slanting rays of morn
When the last star of the night is gone,
Among the woods a doe's first born
Sees the light and begins to stand
In this springtime of mild clime.
Golden sunshine pours forth
Across the woodlands of the earth
Awakening denizens alive and well
After the winters killing frosts.
Deep in glades of rich reserve
Ring out the voices of fauna spry,
Tall grasses and trees reach skyward now
A pleasant mood pervades these warmer days
With whippoorwill music and morning dove songs.
To the quilted pheasant nature talks,

A jack-in-the-pulpit and falcon hawk
As farmers know indicate the time is right
To plant the agricultural fields
As they have done for generations.

Soon the summer is here
Long days and short nights maintain
The growing season's climate
While punctual rain makes moist
The fertile soil. Corn crackles in darkness
In the otherwise silent nocturnal hours,
As well as wheat and barley fields abundant.
When a heat wave hits the town
Cool drinks and watering holes offer
A welcome relief from hothouse weather
Along the sidewalk cafes or out in the country,
In forests far from civilized abodes
Where mountains rise for vacation times,
Or beaches bathe in salt and sand.
Other environments can add retreats
Away from crowds and commercialism
Amid the country's rural avenues
Where countless campsites and tiny cottages
Dot the land, and in hotels
Out on Broadway, or at resort spots
We see the rich and famous
Who also obey nature's laws.

Then, when the summertime is almost over
With warm weather gone for another year
It is back to work and back to school again
Citizens of this thriving town return,
The farmers' sown fields reap ripe harvests
While craftsmen ply their trade in divers ways
Bankers count on money for buying stocks,

Workmen toil hard upon the docks,
Teachers educate students about poets
And men who dream they could haunt
The forest dell still fresh
Where wise men tell their parables.
They know there is a lesson to be learned
In all of this—each day we come a little closer
To ourselves and nature, both together
In one world as mutual friends,
Wise men know there is favor out of this:
To learn new experience and knowledge.
Seasons come and seasons go,
Centuries upon centuries have passed
Since civilization first began,
But looking back on all of it
So little has really changed
In the heart of man.

SWORD AND PEN

Put a sword in his hand and he fights
Put a pen in his hand and he writes,
The legend of Aladdin's lamp,
Or the symbol within Arthur's sword
Genie in a bottle
Sword in a stone
A man's hand is his own,
A man's head is his own,
But his heart is not,
And will not own that which belongs.
Prove I am right
Prove I am wrong
Time will prove all
Mere notes of another song.

WE HAVE GROWN

We have grown
Together
Heart to heart
Head and bone
Love of my life
Be my wife
Before you heart of ice
Is petrified to stone.

DAWN

From the wee hours of the night
Creeps dawn slowly coming on
With an eerie light in the east
Her rosy fingers grow like threads
Into the starry sky as moonlight fades
And the darkness abades,
Clouds turn shades of purple
Venus, the morning star shines
Upon mountain glades in glowing pink haze
Rising in the sky,
A brilliant hue
For early birds to see.
Refulgent light pervades the horizon
As dawn prevails upon the land
In tones of white and blue
The air is cold or cool like night
And dew wets the fields of hay
When the sun breaks through
And sails along the wind
The earth warms to a new day
And morning has begun.

MIDNIGHT

The moon shines brighter than the sun
Burning with fire, reflecting the light
White as an angel, pale as a ghost
Casting shadows on the forest, quiet in the night
Gossamer clouds blow swiftly by,
Illuminated in the sky,
The jet stream carries them away
As lunar interference masks the stars
Which to apogee aspire,
But Polaris shines
Like a beacon in the darkness—a thought
Remembered long ago
In another time, in another place
Born on the fragile wings of ambition
Screaming with desire
The new day yet begun
As geese fly with their song sung
In the distance sounding closer than they are.
How much since then I've changed,
But the heavens are immutable
As are the mysteries of life.
The march of years upon that midnight
In the cool November air
As the November air is cool tonight
At the stroke of twelve in the moonlight
The winds brush against the trees
Which paint an ironic panorama of ideas
Sagacious and wise

Of all that is or ever was
In this world in which we live
So often out of touch with nature,
Thus, so often out of touch with reality.
The picture in my mind is clear
I stare upon the moon in Heaven,
And take solace at midnight when nature sleeps,
It is then I bear the torch for her.

MOTHER NATURE

Alone here in the shady evergreen forest
Where Father Time dances with Mother Nature
I look for her among the needles and the pinecone
Where man has searched in vain since the beginning
High on the waves of the sky jetting
To look down upon her fertile form not forgetting
There on the land were the Black Hills,
A beauty mark on her lovely face,
Sailing over the windy streams
To find colors of mascara and shadow
Encompassing her eyes, lakes crystal and blue,
The mountains were her bosom, snow her bath powder
Newly strewn, whence the seas her bath
Lapping against the limbs of her shore
With the continents her lithe torso,
Lintels of the woodlands in her hair
Colored by the spring and autumn glow
That grows now and forever out of history.

Across the earth I search in vain
Where once I met her long ago
The pure palpable substance
Of an azure eyed, black haired woman
Subtle and true, matriarch to the pragmatist
And the dreamer alike. Wishing to be enthralled
By finding her still fresh
With summer flowers on her cheeks,
I stand alone with the look

Of the lonely and forlorn
Where only the relentless
Power of Time inexorably changes
The face of the earth, but still
Her charm shines through to offer
A bit of generosity in this seemingly
Inanimate, insatiable world.

So nature walks and nature talks
As sweet as night or in daylight
Te burgeon earth, the virid plain
In farmland or fields of grain
The wooded larch, the old, tall tree
Remains the same year after year
Clouds shed a tear and then it is clear
The cleansing rain near the pond rife
With aquatic plants and wildlife.
So when it is time to grow strong
Remember she can do no wrong.
Nature's haunts are quiet places
Where we can hide self-conscious faces
And in the glades the forces laid
Upon this earth when given birth
Seem to halt in woodlands deep
To find no faults on mountains steep
In blue, cool lakes fishermen cast
With poles as tools, these days will last
'Til seasons circle the year round
And children walk on holy ground.

Here is to Mother Nature
And those times of long ago
When the sun was never setting
And the clouds were n'er in view,
Gregarious and fun she was

True to her heritage of God
When the day was never done.
Her ken was very lofty
She flew like a bird in the sky
Time has treaded softly
Upon her ancient brow
The trees wave to her allegiance
With the leaves of every spring,
In summertime on the wing
Her songbirds always sing.
The fall another season
Only she knows her father's reason,
The winter a time for slumbers
Her harvest is the lumber
Of trees grown tall with riches
Of the soil and the rain.
Her dress sometimes is plain
When the woods are barren,
But always is she friendly
Though seldom with a modest heart,
These years have been a charmer
And my thoughts of her return
If she thinks of me I know
Our separation will not be long.
She is grudgeless and perfect
And wise in all affairs
Her law is that of justice
Inviolate through the years.

I have searched from sky to Heaven
I know who she is
Sometimes her memory falters,
But her course she never alters
From monarchy and reign,
Her life is one of romance

Father Time she will meet again
Though eons come and go
Through wind, hail, sleet, and snow
She conquers her possessor
Who will not hold her forever,
Thus, for now she does not let go,
Her origin he will never know.

RAINBOW LIGHT AND THE HUMAN SPECTRUM

Phoebus Apollo rises from his slumbers
As light dawns on the horizon of consciousness
Pointing the obelisk of his sundial
With ever present shadow to the west.
Under the ceiling of the chamber of space
And the vault of the mansion of Heaven,
Apollo's chariot, Perseus led
Races with tireless power towards
His predetermined destination among
The ever-passing highways of the wind.
Helios transcends his wispy mask of clouds,
Throws himself headlong into the fray
Across the pristine azure seeking zenith
To the torrents of a rainbow's cascade
Of spring prisms painted on the bejeweled air
Through the facets, faces of the droplets
Refracting and projecting into beauty
All the colors of the human spectrum.

The virtue and purity of a maiden
Is Heaven sent, like the white hue
Of fair-weather cotton ball clouds
Floating on the lavender ocean of the skies,
Budding pink is the carnation of youth,
Ocher, the color of adolescence, like
That of a chameleon, blush rouge

Is on a young lady's face, enamored
And vivacious. Playing on the brown
Cool earth, forest animals and travelers
Guided by Olympian spirits enshrined
With the pride of silver, bronze, and golden
Accoutrements and the Tyrian purple
Of their noble murex sashes,
The viridescence of Dryad tree nymphs,
The flaxen glowworm hair of threshers in the fields,
The gray gaiety of Cyllene the moon;
Orange happiness shines on the face of love
Growing blue with sadness as years march on,
Sometimes green with the envy of a woodsman
Who sees a scarlet saucy damsel in a carriage
Red with anger at her beaux
For too much violet and lilac passion
Often with craven yellow,
But, alas, as the colors of humanity go
They all turn black in the end
And then course down to the cerulean ocean
Of forever.

LIGHT I-POINTS OF LIGHT

Points of light
Expanding into rays
Reflecting, refracting
Penetrating waves,
Glow in the darkness
Of the unknown
Shedding enlightenment
On the masses
Bringing warmth
To the soul
Of the untold multitudes.

LIGHT II-WHEN ON THIS EARTH WE SEE YOUR GRACE

When on this earth we see your grace
Pervading all things good and wonderful,
The years pass, you are the same
As people age in time and space
There is no force that thwarts you
Eons have passed since you began
From Heaven born. Changes on earth
Are transient compared to you
Immutable and eternal light,
Your vision and speed
Will last forever in our eyes.
Like from the sun you come
And like to the clouds you go,
Light, you greet us every day at dawn,
And when night comes you say good-bye
Until the following morn, as it has been,
As it will always be.

LIGHT III-SOMETIMES THERE'S PLENTY OF IT

Sometimes there's plenty of it
Sometimes it is so rare,
It costs nothing in the country
It costs nothing at the fair,
You can't buy it at the grocers
You can't buy it at the store,
It weighs nothing on the scale
It is a physic's law,
And when it is you need it
It always seems to be there
So remember whence it comes
And remember whither it goes
And though it may be hiding
And though it may take some finding
You'll know it when you see it
Because everywhere it glows.
Light IV-In the Infinite Cosmos
In the infinite cosmos
Lay the chasmal abyss of the imprimordial,
Silent and foreboding.
Before time began lay the infernal creation
Sprung from the eternal darkness
Where the gods of Heaven sped
Floating on the etheral wind
Where the empyrean convulsed
With the heart that pulsed

Along with the holy ring
Of angelic hosts that sweetly sing
The coming of an immortal thing.
So went the seraphs this way and that
All with two eyes that could not see,
They prayed to the high omniscient deity
To carve light from the void,
And when light came and God saw
The good he'd done, he blessed the earth,
And gave us light along with warmth,
Return to grace, and Jesus' birth.

LIGHT V-LIGHT WITH YOUR MAGNETIC ATTRACTIVENESS

Light with your magnetic attractiveness
And electrifying personality
Traveling so fast through vacuum's emptiness
Shining on us with alacrity,

Illuminating all by the fireside
Casting into the shadows
Your brilliance where none can hide,
Beaming bright through morning windows.

Often something comes from nothing
When you're a piece of light,
And often nothing comes from something
It is all nature's delight.

You weigh so little light
Compared to a particle heavy
By the time we look you're out of sight
You move so fast and quickly.

You're flying at the limit
At all told breakneck speed
By the time we get to measure it
You have a positron conceived.

Light by the physicist's clock
Cannot be beat in any race
There is no way to make it stop
Only a neutrino can keep pace.

When you're a light pulse flying
From the sun or nearby star
Your spectrum is not plying
A red shift from afar.

And when it comes to gravitation
Your little photon bends
Like when you see a proton
The physicist apprehends,

And when you're done creating
Energy plants eat
We will soon be waiting
For your infrared heat.

So when you think of light
And the strange stuff that it is made of
Try to keep it in sight
Because it brings the warmth we love.

ECLECTIC I

Love will never be the same
The glow of passion's flame
Begins dimmer and dimmer to grow
With passing years of dearth and famine
And empty hearted haughtiness
You will learn to know all your
Hand and body language
Along with the demon in your fiery eyes,
Certain, sure, infallible
Symbols of tempered passion
Damned to the dungeons of diabolic
Vanities of critical faculty.

Roses, red roses are buzzing with bees
Loading their combs with golden grained pollen
Led by rich odors wafted on the breeze
Brimmed 'til they're filled with sweet nectar laden
Rose ephemeral, perennial springs
Up from the earth under the gleaming sun
Each spring, each morn are dewdrops glistening
On leaves enduring when the fresh flowers come
As will my tears for you my pretty rose
In these weak lines when youth to palsy grows.

ECLECTIC II

Lady Luck is dancing with the spirit of the age,
God or goddess lurking in the soul of man
Imply robust and pagan deities
Flaying and flailing Delphic rites
For a thrust of bacchanalian dances.

For He leadeth the blind and the ageless
Wisdom not into the cyclone of chaos,
But from the hands of callous temptation.

Mysteries of locked embraces
And flurries of glorious caresses
Spring amongst locks and tresses.

ECLECTIC III

Ye denizens of grand and classic mold
'Tis a tid or bit of poesy I've composed
To offer up libations right and quick
Ere wolves have had their fill of finest pick;
Zeus, Apollo, Aphrodite, Helen,
The boughs and bowers once of nightly heaven
Now caverns and of coves where Charon poles
Along the Styx to Acheron's repose
Among the endless labyrinths and canals
The deposed clique awaits, the muse arouse
Them from antiquity's infernal realm
To beg and choose a master for the helm.
All of Attica's most favorite sages
Immortalized, wit on ageless pages
Propose in idlings, the pith in portent
The ancients bequeathed in fortune fated
To be rich in pure wisdom, forever unjaded.

ECLECTIC IV

Above the flickering tongues of the flame of life
One above all others stood my own
Mind, which pulsed
Not to the rhythm of my entity
But to the image of another self
Whom or which I took within to heart
As a being more worthy of all good than any else.
How shall I call thee? By any other
Name thou art, though all the same
Thou art a sacred blessing and a fatal curse
Thou art the first and last from beginning unto end
Few have there been that answer to your name.
Love was a thing that came in the night
And slept with us there while we dreamed vivid sights,
Love was a thing that left not a day
'Til swept away, overthrown, reborn
Inexorably changed and never regained.

Come hell or high water
Come rain, sleet, snow
With a backbreaking burden
By the sweat of my brow
Time will n'er conquer
The immutable resolve
Of a perpetual vow.

ECLECTIC V

The candle of a life illuminates
The darkness of oblivion's abyss
As a tallow beacon to the depths
Upon the wellspring's opaque waters;
The rope is unwound, the bucket lowered
Into the mouth of Athena's basin.

THE TIDE IS HIGH

The tide is high, the moon is full
The stars are bright, the sky is clear
Today was warm so is tonight
My love is deep, but she's not here
To be with me and hold me tight.

SCYTHE OF THE REAPER

Despise not the Scythe of the Reaper
Though his Sickle in time
Sows fallen faggots
To stoke the fire
Of Phaedra's pyre
In protestations to grieving
Cassandra who
Forecasting unseen disaster
Now denies she ever knew her.

Despise not the Reaper
Above the grim sky
Once I did sail,
For beneath the weary ether
His granite tombstone
With this emblem engraved:
A bas-relief scene
Of kernels of grain
Of wheat, barley, malt, hops, and rye,
All swept awry
From the plain
By the Air
By the sweeper in Rain
On the shoulders of Clouds
To the steps of the Sun and the Moon.
Hand in hand may they ride
The stallion of purebred rhyme,

The Reaper of Time
And the sweeper in Rain.

Wake not the Sleeper
Rest needs his slumbers
Undisturbed in repose
Snoring a saw
Though cutting no trails
But the formless details
Captured in the labyrinths
And catacombs
By the Nexus—sleep
Is not blind
But the leader of sheep
Who have stepped
Time after Time
'Til they wore out their soles.

SUNSET

Gazing at the sunset
Under a pink and russet sky
Now with the horizon met
Daylight begins to die.

The sun takes its repose
Ready for another night
All wonder where it goes
As darkness replaces light.

The colors are most joyous,
But the hues begin to fade
As we all peer to the west
Where the giant orb is laid.

Some peaceful twilight moments
Atop a mountainside,
Seen are the sun's last movements
As he runs to hide.

The sun at rest this evening
Setting on this day,
The stars and moon are waiting
For the light to go away.

THOSE EYES

Those eyes sparkle
Like stars in the night
Those blue orbs beckon
Pleasure and delight.

AUDIENCE

You are the audience
Behind your own eyes,
And the world
Is an amphitheater.

MILK THE BREEZE

Her eyes spoke
Through the nether night
And the imprimordial darkness,
And I heard her.

DREAMS AND REMEMBRANCES

YOU MAKE ME HAPPY

You make me happy
You make me sad
You are everything
I ever had,
You make me giggle
You make me mad
Our times together
Were not bad.
You make me soft
You make me hard
When we were in love
You made me glad,
You made me come
You made me go
Now in distant places
Many years ago,
So if you ever read this poem
Remember the faces
You have seen.
Between now and then
When we first met
A long time has come.
Some things change
And some do not
With others I've been

And they made me grin,
But when the day is done
You're the one
Still in my heart.

RETREAT

While aves settle at dusk
On tender leaves and blooming buds
The final chirps and chatter end
Almost abruptly with light's wane,
As an overcast Ithacan sky
Retreats to a rainy eve.

ID

The ideals of the superego
Pertains only in conjunction
To gratification of the id.
The ego is a masked protection
Of the unconsciously directed will.

SPANISH MAIN

Pirates on a ship of fools
Kidnap our unwitting souls
And mince tough meaty truths
With a sharp cutlass tongue
Edging the scabbard's tooth,
Captured the gullible young
In the cruel domineering
And remorseless clutches
Of blatant buccaneering
Inculcating wenches
With implied insinuation
That a solemn sea of mercy
Lies 'neath a shark infested shoal.

SWORD IN A STONE

Put a sword in his hand and he fights,
Put a pen in his hand and he writes.
I am the sword and I am the pen
And she the stone, true ever is she only to her health
All else in me she damns
By the words of her foul mouth
Which reveals her inner self
As the source of her needs,
But not the object of her love
She endorsed in pleas,
"You make my life miserable."
There is a single source
That dwells in any mention
Of the word love which raising your attention
Retains the lame sound I cry, "Remorse."
Only love breeds birth
Love is the only wealth
Life needs to flourish,
Life gives to life, hand to mouth,
Love is the only pure wealth
That flowers in a flourish of blessed birth.
Your curses are my acclaim
Your lie of hate
Will not damp the flame
Of my heart
In memory to your face
Which veils a mine
Not bedazzled by, but at war

With the untapped vein
That grows from a heart
That glows like a worm
That glows out of turn,
But stays in a cave
Bathing not in a warm
Canopy of sun, but
In the dark shadow of a dank stone.
Within the untapped vein
Lies the secret of desire
That marches on
Despite control
Or conscious ire
Under reign of my visage.
If your imagination
Is to you commendable
Then do not deny
Knowing your own heart
And its location.
That is the only truth you will decry
Within yourself in spite
Of surface lies
That smile all is best,
All is all that every day has seen
A girl who to my face
Profanes her own birth
With claims she does
Not comprehend the meaning
Of obscene.
I sound the same and will not change
My voice in silence
My lineament in silhouette
Cursed by vain lusts
As no quality
Retains the memory lost

In the generality of whereabouts
By the general popularity
Of ideas
That we are a family
Born of one source
Embarked on a quest
Of idolatries
Not of idle vulgarities.
Wave of all waves
Heart of all hearts
Love is the truth my life
Has borne for one whose
Adolescent years are gone
From all the days
Remaining still to give
Me life I, single,
Sing a song
Of a sword stuck in a stone
Of a girl whose heart
Was made of glass
Then when broken
By a sword revealed
The coldest blast
Of anger, arrogance, and rage
That ever in one soul
Unleashed Pandora's box
Upon God's honest truth
That I in words avow.

ETERNAL FLAME

Cast not about the wind
For the wind shall blow
Feeding the eternal flame
That burns
One and the same
For John Fitzgerald Kennedy.
Not a leader of many,
But a leader of us all,
For what few years you ruled
We will remember
By the strength of your heart
And the symbol of your eternal flame.
We will remember
How you fought for freedom
And your country
In the face of foreign danger
You did not blink,
But faced it down without blinking.
At home in America
In which I live
Burns the eternal flame
Symbol of your life
Cut short in its prime,
Burns the eternal flame
Symbol of your Camelot.
May your flame burn forever.
In death
As in life your works shall last;

Freedoms we have
Because of you
That no despot can undo,
No one knows how great you were
And no one knows how great you would have been,
Your decisiveness and determination,
Your confidence and consistency
In world and human affairs
Was beyond that of mortal men.
So may the eternal flame
Burn forever on your grave
And may the wind that blows
And may the rain that falls
And may many seasons' snows
Not extinguish thee
Your eternal flame
A tribute to your memory
And to your legacy
That shall last throughout history.

PRESENCE

Presence—image
Of spiritual force
Still the dream I wish for,
Cynically profaning
The Swiss music box of my heart
Yet ever retaining
The key to its source.

DEEP

Deep in the steep'd dusky stacks
Down on the dank shadowy steps
Worn in the stone, smooth impressions;
The trudge of forgotten votaries,
A carved memorial this unwritten communication
To future scholars of endless questioning.

WHAT I HAVE SEEN

I've seen blue eyes and many blondes
I've seen spring flowers and summer sun
I've seen waterfalls and big azure skies
I've seen canyons great and colorful
I've seen the desert sands
I've seen grottoes with stalagmites shiny
I've seen tall, medium, and short models
On TV, in magazines, in all their glory
I've seen autumns and winters hoary
I've seen the snows with their quiet beauty
I've felt love and I've felt the touch
I've felt embraces and I've felt the clutch.
So goes my life with all its strife
I've seen my friends take up a wife
I sit here and wonder why
Some live long while others die,
I've seen just about all it takes
To find the truth, to find the fakes,
But in all the years that have
Come and gone
I've seen no one so truly
In love, passion, and youthful beauty.

TEARS FOR YESTERDAY

Along the lonely path we crossed
With stars in our eyes
And remorse upon our tongues,
We each had our diversions
We each had our white lies
We each loved one another
Till circumstances did arise,
We could not be together
We cannot be together now.
The years have drifted slowly
With solitude and thought
No word comes about you
No word I have sought,
But in my mind's eye remains
The beauty of your sight
With but a silent cry
For what little is left to say,
We went our separate way
Leaving tears for yesterday.

FROM MOTHER TO SON

I was there when your life was begun
And I loved you when you were young
I love you still to this very day
With all the trials and tribulations we've been through
Just remember I love you.
So in the future think of me
If there is anything I can do
To help you in hard times
I'll always be here for you
Your mother tried and true.

CLOUDS

Soaring above the noisy land
Quietly passing always grand
Changing shape and color; first white then gray
In evening streaming down a ray
Through clouds purple, violet, and blush pink
The sun begins to sink
Pouring forth from between their veils
Falling on the greenest swales.

Gathering quickly one summer afternoon
Eclipsing the sun in all his grandeur, soon
Great, tall anvil-headed, dark
Quelling the song of the meadowlark
Ominous with thunder and lightning
Sounding like great armies fighting
Impressed against the sky's background
Storm clouds form and rain does pound
A powerful display of nature's strength
As rivers overflow their banks
The storm surges winds blow fierce
Lightning through the sky does pierce
The clouds with a thunderous din
The heavens wide appear to open
Rain beats down on ford and field
Just as quickly the storm does yield
Rain stops, winds dissipate, and then
Fair-weather clouds return again.

A cloudless sky we see some day,
But we know they are not far away
In summer bringing rain to water farms
In winter bringing snow to bare trees' open arms
In spring a cooling shower and a beautiful rainbow
In autumn nor'easters and sometimes hurricanes
Hanging low
Clouds come and clouds go all the time
With vintner's grapes or hoary rime
We see clouds floating, cotton-balls overhead
Clouds make the sunrise orange and the sunset red
And though so often we wish to see blue skies
We know that clouds will come again with the rain
That Heaven cries.

THE CURSE OF HATHOR

These secret magic potions
That make men's hearts beat fast
And give a crazy notion
That a witch's love will last
Drunk on love and passion
The spirit of the mind
Transfigured by hypnosis
Unaltered throughout time
The cryptic, sinister purpose
And the banal drops in wine
The sorcerer will not surrender
The bottle or its source
To love she does pretend more
Her speech is never coarse
But remember what we came for—to beat
A curse much worse.

The years have taken many
And many more will come
Manifest and plenty
Before its days are done
Searching for the beauty
In a woman's eyes
Who is to know her magic
Would make men cheat and lie
In a life turned tragic
In turmoil so they die
These years unrequited

These years of pensive talk
Some say they will not try it
Some only take a walk
But another in another's arms
Will replenish lovers' charms
So take what we can get
And remember don't forget.

THE PAINTED DESERT

The morning sun breaks on the red horizon
Where the eagle flies from the rocky ledge
Dawn, crowned in glory, all dressed in crimson
As the snake like a river slithers in the sedge.
Rising over the parched desert landscape
Brilliant reflections of magenta haunt the rocks
Sharp, jagged silhouettes are cast across lakes
Hemmed in by dams and pleasure boat docks
Painted on the country like some prehistoric scene
Are the colors of which the Indians dream.

This is the Painted Desert of antique fame
Where hunters come to capture its beauty
Armed with cameras and easels on the barren plain
Stealing pictures of nature for futurity
The high precipice with stone outcroppings
The low valleys with yellow sand
Are visitors with sights amazing
Upon the dry and infertile land
Where the sun beats down all day long
And the vulture's screech is the only song.

Images of shadows mix in the midday sun
While sightseers stop to view the surroundings,
A tarantula along the road where coyotes run
Cacti and scrub brush the only plants there abounding.
A yearly spring rain is all that falls here
Rapidly gathering its precipitation in torrents

Which soon fade in the heat and brightness sere
Leaving life in fresh flowers for the briefest of moments
Cloudless skies fill the air before sunset
In dusty hues of gold and ruby dark russet.

Dust rises from the floor of the wasteland
And settles in the atmosphere at eve
Whipped up by the winds of eons grand
That sculpt the rocks and mountains cleave
As dusk travels before twilight arrives
The sunset sparkles in yellow, pink, and purple
That orange ball on the glowing land implies
Darkness will be here with starlight ample,
At night the owl hunts for creatures nocturnal
With nature in the right, her laws supernal.

Now taking leave in the dry nighttime chill
Desert fox, panther and other carnivores revel
In the quiet xerothermic air so still
About which the environment seems sterile
Constellations up above shining bright
The Milky Way, a swath across the sky
Our sleepy eyes await the morning light
And to another day we say good-bye,
Good-bye, oh Painted Desert of ancient fame
Thy beauty and thy splendor shall not wane.

THE SORCERER'S INCANTATION

He weaves a magic spider web
In words of a demonic language
No one seems to know
With a falcon's feather quill
And octopus' poison ink
Upon a young ewe's skin
Beyond the sight of man
In a timeless vortex
Where ageless still they grow
These spells of the occult
Invoke the winters' snow
Which to seers are portentous
Of angry storms a-blow
That leaves men seeking pleasure
Their fate tossed to the winds
Where destiny is haunted
By the Lethe's flow
With the bane of many victims
In carnage and in throes
They fall upon the biers
And the fires lay them low.

So a witch's hex is conjured
There its woogie stews
In caldrons deep and distant
In lands of long ago

The ancient potion brews
Love and evil deeds
Entering the sanguine veins
These passing years foregone
Where the nepenthe never leaves
The shady mortal souls
For many have been stricken
And many omens seen,
The incantation's forces
In the nether regions
And in chthonic, forlorn caves
Lurk with the sorcerer's curses
And the powers that they hold
As the hypnotic motions
Of a gypsy's dream unfolds.

ROOT

Though every root grows not a tree
Every tree must grow from root
Though every heart grows not new love
Every love is born at heart.
Though every man must have a heart
And every heart must have a love to grow
And every love must have a heart to know
An empty heart still keeps in root a bough.

LAMENTS

For the love of a little girl
I come trekking through these lonely halls
And when I find that she's not here
I write laments on dirty walls.

If I in a sunny dale were deeped
And you should come dancing, prancing by
You would to my stone your coldest cheek
Turn, and make all our heavens cry.

As the flood waters rise up around
A man in a boat hears your scream,
And carried to sea laden ground
You'll anchor with the tall and the lean.

HIGH COUNTRY

The photoelectric energetic sun
Spins her golden rays across
An autumnal earth. Endless days
Set over and over again
With a western sky casting shadows
Upon the deep valleys from the hills
And mountain rifts. A sere wind
Licks parched leaves on the forest's
Carpet as a raccoon scurries
From his home in a hollow
Tree stump to other more accommodating
Environs.

The photogenic sun shines forth
At daybreak where dry leaves rest
Beneath our tent, the wind crosses
The placid pools of a cool stream,
A deep breath of fresh morning air
Tingles our rubescent cheeks on this trek
To reach uncharted territory
In the high country.

FRAT BOY

Rock-and-roll and brew the way the song goes
You asked to drink the white stuff from my hose
They say I'm just a DJ with a song,
But I for one know they are far from wrong,
Monster party lunatic on the lawn
Everybody 'til the sun comes up dawn
All out in the dark her band plays along
You hear the singer moan every now and again
Out in the dark laughing over the time,
But the missing new moon masks me in dark
So let's do it now while we're here in the park,
I'm hard as a rock and tired of talk
So why don't we go for a little walk
And find a comfortable spot we can lay
And talk pillow talk 'til the break of day.

THE CHAUVINIST

Choose me now
Or choose me again
The choice is yours
In the end.
The choice is yours
Don't let me down
Lift me up off of the ground
Let me take you round the town
Let me love you on soft ground
Just let me tell you
Don't make a sound.

FROM THE HEART

Long ago in times unknown
There lived a couple
I don't recall
They were the all
Of us until today
When we come
A new day's breath
Unto the fall
When once again
I will call
You on the phone
To start anew
The love of you.

Long ago in times I know
We lived a couple
I recall
We were the all
And again that day
When we come
A new life will breathe
By the next fall
When again I call
Upon you to give
To start anew
The love of you.

A SIMPLE THOUGHT FROM LONG AGO

Love is truth,
Pure, simple, free
In all walks of life
Happy to be in the heart
Husband and wife
I see everything beautiful
Topaz eyes in dreams surreal
What all adore, admire, implore
With seasons unchanging reflections remain
In mirror, in water still, her image the same
Teardrop blue cerulean rue.

MEETING IN THE EVENING

A vivid sunset robes the evening sky,
Shades of orange, pink, and purple fly
Across the firmament's empyrean crown
In this fine suburban town.

The dusky colors gleam in the pallid light
As the moon glows golden in the harboring night,
Songbirds in the wood chant proudly
Peregrinating sparrows hissing loudly.

Two lovers meet in the empty park
Accompanied by the sound of the evening lark
Traffic lights and neon signs light up
They join each other over a coffee cup.

The fertile moon garbed in clouds of gray
The city's nightlife in suave display
Restaurants and movies everywhere
With the scent of perfume in her hair.

The lovers stroll much as any couple
Holding hands with affection ample
Her face like a diadem of beauty
With ardent thoughts deep and moody.

Sweet talk and laughter drift in the air
Amid the clack of cars with incessant blare,

The coffeehouse fills with the usual crowd
The regulars come but do not talk loud.

It begins to grow late, about half past ten
The lovers fill their mugs again
Closing time comes with a hug
And business-like patrons packages lug.

Each has their own place to go,
But they to each other do not say, "No."
They retreat to a tavern up the street
Each has for one another a special treat.

After hours in the humid darkness
They are waiting without drunkenness
Around about midnight or later
A gentleman thinks he'd like to date her.

He is too late, they've already left
With his personality she is impressed
A little get-together at her place
And when it's morn he'll leave in haste.

A businessman's work never ends
And she a career woman, tends
To her job before friends
As into her cherished moments he blends.

THE SPIRIT OF
TUTANKHAMEN

resume the spirit of king tut
is left untouched hand in hand
with a lotus blossom on the face
of amenhensen (ankhensenamen).

the tomb of amenhensen is there
for the love of god is always there
for her eternal love she waits there
eternally true.

ITALIAN ICE

You can keep that rich ice cream
Italian ice is what I dream
Bitter blue's my favorite flavor
But there's no time off for good behavior
Italian ice so very cold
While I sit here just growing old.

NOWHERE

Play me a song to remember you by
When I in a barren desert must walk
With nothing but earth and a painted sky
To hear me choke on my misguided talk.

A red subset's burning, painting the way
I should have traveled perhaps long ago
Still something I feel beckons me to say
Please spare a few words even to say, "No."

PARKWAY SOUTH

Parkway South where I want to be
On the road for you and me
At the Jersey shore so fun
A shame our love never once begun
To bear the fruit of which it should
I would have loved you if I could.

Parkway South where I want to go
Driving fast or driving slow
If my statue reaches not your Locust tree
I'll never find another one like thee
Around every curve and every bend
I come to realize I'll never see you again.